Grand Diplôme® Cooking Course

Volume 19

The Story of Wine

by C. F. Turgeon

A Danbury Press Book

Contents

The Danbury Press

a division of Grolier Enterprises Inc.

Robert B. Clarke Publisher
Anne Willan Editor
Mark Cherniavsky Assistant Editor

Library of Congress Catalog Card Number: 72-13896
© Phoebus Publishing Company/BPC Publishing
Limited, 1971/1972/1979
Filmsetting by Petty and Sons Ltd., Leeds, England.
Printed in the United States of America

4567899

PICTURE CREDITS

We would like to thank the Wine and Spirit Education Trust Ltd., London for their help, and for the pictures on the following pages: 12, 13, 16, 17, 18, 24, 25, 32, 33, 44, 45, 46, 52, 54, 62, 65, 66, 67, 78, 88. Food from France provided the maps of France and pictures (© C.N.V.F. Sopexa) on the following pages: 13, 23, 30, 34, 35, 36, 37, 43, 47, 48, 57, 64, 72, and the French Commissariat Generale de Tourisme provided those on pages 20, 55, 71. Picturepoint, London provided pictures on pages 11, 22, 26, 38, 74, 79, 82, 83, 84, 86, 90, 102, 103. Michael Holford, London provided the pictures on pages 4, 39, 40, 41, 56, 80, 99, Spectrum those on pages 76, 77, 81, 85, The Mansell Collection, those on pages 19 and 68, John Watney those on pages 61 and 69, Giraudon, Paris the Limbourg brothers picture on pages 58–59. The pictures on pages 140–142 were especially commissioned from David Levin, London. The California Wine Institute provided the pictures on pages 99, 101, 103, 104, 105, 106, 107, 109, 111, 114, 115, 116, 120, 121, 122, 123, 124, 125, 127, 129, 131, 132, 134. The Author's pictures appear on pages 74, 100, 102, 108, 110, 112, 113, 115, 126, 128, 133, 135, 136. The picture on page 137 is from the Greyton H. Taylor Wine Museum.

Suddenly everyone's crazy about wine. Ten years ago in this country, it sat sullenly on liquor store shelves; now retailers can't keep enough in stock. In their rush to buy wine, Americans are discovering two things: first, that despite wine's disarming simplicity in the glass, it is easy to be confused when confronting those rows of bottles in a good wine shop; second, that the enormous new demand for wine is pushing prices higher and higher.

So short a book as this can only afford an overview of the world of wine. But it can try to clear away much of the confusion about where wine comes from, how it is made, why some wines are considered superior and what the words on a wine label really mean. It can also steer you to those less recognized wine producing areas where you may still find good quality for price.

Because this volume has been written for a North American audience, the coverage of U.S. wines is more extensive than in most similar works. This is only proper, since nine out of ten glasses of wine drunk in the U.S. come from American vineyards. Moreover, this extra attention is timely in view of the recent significant advances in the quality and output of American wine.

Finally, this book differs from many in emphasizing more about how wines are made than predicting how they will taste in the glass. This approach was chosen in the belief that the person who knows the basic roles played by the grape, the sun, the soil and the winemaker in vineyards around the world will have greater understanding and enjoyment from the wines he drinks. As for explaining how wine tastes, there is really only one qualified spokesman: yourself.

A votre santé,

Charles F. Turgeon

The Story of Wine

PART I:

Wine History
Wine Making

THE HISTORY OF WINE

A stele with a representation of Baal with grapes. From Carthage, North Africa

No matter how far we look back into man's history there seems to be evidence that he knew how to extract the juice from grapes and ferment it. The basic procedure is so simple that it seems safe to assume that wine was man's first alcoholic drink and it probably originated around 6,000 B.C. in the cradle of civilization somewhere between the eastern end of the Mediterranean and India. Most likely, the transformation of grape juice into wine first occured when someone left several bunches of wild grapes in a pottery jar. Fermentation, which is simply the natural conversion of plant sugar into alcohol, would have begun spontaneously as soon as yeast spores on the grape skins made contact with the sweet juices oozing from the fresh fruit.

By 3,000 B.C. there is clear evidence that wine grapes were being widely cultivated in the eastern Mediterranean lands now known as Egypt, Syria and Lebanon. Later, the Greeks imported grapes to make wine and they gradually gained a knowledge of viniculture which spread through the Mediterranean basin.

But if the Greeks were the wine teachers of the ancient world, it was the Romans who really set about making wine the typical European beverage. By the time the Roman Empire was at its height, vineyards had been established not only in much of Italy, but also in France, Germany, England and in several parts of eastern Europe and even southern Russia. The Romans undoubtedly had an unerring eye for the right place to plant grapes. Beginning in the first century A.D., they started vineyards in the Rhône Valley, then the principal route into France from the Mediterranean. By the second century A.D., wine-growing had reached the area just north of the Rhône (between Lyons and Dijon), now known as Burgundy. By the third century, the Romans had established vineyards in the Loire Valley and not long thereafter in Champagne and in Germany's Rhine Valley.

With the fall of the Roman Empire, winemaking might have vanished along with the other civilized crafts of Europe. Fortunately, there was one institution which was relatively unharmed by the invasions of the barbarians and the breakdown in public order which followed: the Church. Throughout the Dark and Middle Ages, it acted as the custodian of the language, arts and interests of the Roman world, and these included winemaking.

The Church had at least two reasons for preserving viniculture. First, wine was essential to the central sacrament of the Christian faith: Holy Communion. Second, it was a source of income. Many of the famous vineyards of the present day were protected and cultivated by various Catholic orders from the fall of the Roman Empire to the time of the French Revolution. In an age when men spent as much time fighting as farming, the Church lands were islands of tranquility in which grapes could be grown and turned into wine.

Van Riebeeck planted the first vineyards in South Africa in the 17th century

Wine in the New World

When the nation-states of modern Europe began to emerge in the 15th century, their rulers showed an interest in discovering new continents to which they could transport their culture and from which they could gather new wealth. The discovery of the New World and sea routes to Africa and Asia was followed by waves of emigration from the European continent. Wine was basic to the way of life of many of these emigrants and thus it is no surprise that, wherever conditions permitted, one of the first priorities in their new settlements was the planting of vineyards.

This natural inclination to plant wine grapes often had official backing. The Spanish expeditions to Mexico, for example, were chartered with the goal of establishing new sources of wine as well as mineral treasure. These ventures, and others undertaken by Portugal, brought

Bishop Odo blessing wine. From the Bayeux tapestry, 11th century

viniculture to the New World in the 16th Century. Vineyards were first planted in Mexico about 1525 and had also been set out in parts of Argentina and Peru before 1600. Before the end of the 1700s, winemaking had spread into North America near what was to become the city of San Diego, California.

Wine grapes were planted in South Africa by Dutch settlers in the 1650s and later by Protestant refugees from France. The Napoleonic wars gave South African vintners their chance to become major producers by denying the British their usual sources of wine in France. English settlement of Australia began in the late 1700s and grape vines were aboard on the first ships. Wine was produced near Sydney before the turn of the century and by the 1830s the foundations for Australian viniculture were firmly established.

Wine in Modern Europe

The wine industries started in the Americas, Africa and Australia during the colonial era are only now coming into their full maturity and their importance will grow further. Nonetheless, Europe is likely to remain the center of viniculture. It is blessed with an ideal grape-growing environment. Its vintners have long experience with every aspect of winemaking and can take credit for most of the major advances which man has made in vine-tending and winemaking.

Perhaps the single most important European contribution to the improvement of wine since Roman days has been the invention of the cork. Until the 18th century, wines spoiled rather quickly because the ceramic jars, goat-skin bags and wooden barrels in which they were stored were hard to keep airtight. Glass bottles had long been avail-

able, but their traditional stoppers — rags soaked in olive oil and wooden plugs coated with pine pitch — failed to protect the wine from air and often tainted it with extraneous flavors.

An effective seal was not discovered until the early 1700s when the flexible inner bark of a Spanish cork tree was first used. Vintners soon found that cork not only offered a means of preventing spoilage, but that wine stored in air-tight bottles took on an entirely new character as it aged. The simple aroma of fermented grape juice, given time to quietly mature, was found to develop a perfumed scent or 'bouquet,' and gained a smoothness and a subtlety of flavor not previously known.

It is in fact, fair to say that the adoption of the cork in the 1700s separated the wines of the ancient world from those of today.

A map of the vineyards of Europe

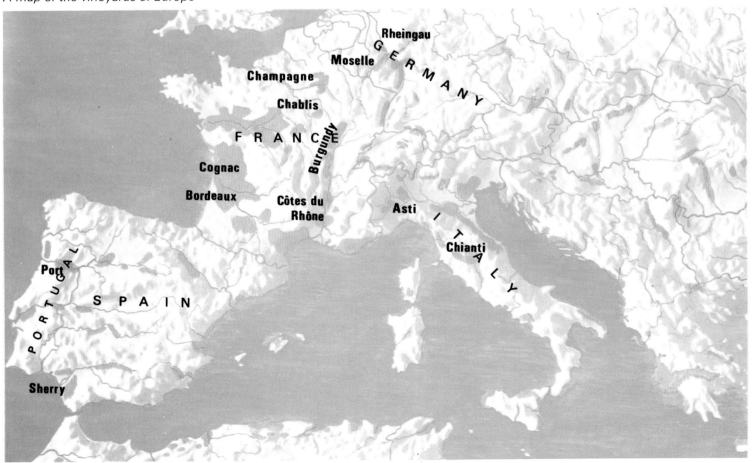

The Phylloxera disaster

This discovery was followed in the 19th century by a disaster which threatened for a time to destroy European viniculture. The roots of grape vines were attacked on an epidemic scale by soil lice called *phylloxera vastatrix*. The disease seems to have originated in North America and was probably transmitted to Europe around the 1850s when U.S. vintners brought their native vines to Europe to exchange for the classic varieties with which they hoped to improve their infant wine industry. What became known as the phylloxera plague swept across Europe with devastating speed.

Vineyards were flooded, burned and covered with chemicals, but nothing seemed to protect the treasured vines. Finally, growers took the radical course of importing more vines from the U.S. and grafting what remained of their classic stock to the American plants. It worked; ages ago, American vine roots had developed an immunity to the phylloxera louse and European vines could be grafted to these immune roots without significantly affecting their vinous character.

Today, virtually all the vines in Europe have been laboriously grafted onto American root stock. To a certain extent the world is still feeling the effects of the phylloxera plague because in the price of virtually every bottle of wine is included the cost of grafting.

The present day

The story of wine in the 20th century has been marred by wars fought over some of the prime vineyards of Europe and by the curtailment of America's taste for wine as a result of Prohibition. But, for the most part, it is a tale of steadily improving quality and extraordinary growth in popularity. Never has more wine been made and made so well as in the present era.

If there is a cloud on the horizon, it is the growing disparity between the world's supply of good wine and the demand for it. The popularity of wine is growing so fast, particularly in the U.S., that there is simply not enough good wine to go around. The resulting inflation in wine prices has been aggravated by the entry of speculators into the wine market who have made large purchases of wine which they withhold from immediate sale. For the most part, this hoarding involves only the most prestigious wines. But the speculation has had an inflationary effect on the entire market, hurting those consumers who simply purchase wines for pleasure. The average customer's best defense is to avoid the expensive, famous wine names and to learn to recognize wines which suit his taste as well as his budget.

This chart shows the major wine-producing nations of the present day according to their output in gallons and also indicates the quantities of wine they import and consume:

The Leading Vinicultural Nations 1977				
Country	**Production** 1,000 US Gallons	**Imports** 1,000 US Gallons	**Consumption** 1,000 US Gallons	US Gallons per capita
Italy	1,692,654	6,287	1,479,936**	26,34**
France	1,382,850	171,030	1,412,835	26.66
USSR	845,376	49,788	908,779**	3.54**
Spain	604,972	291	528,941	17.17
Argentina	655,483	†	611,788	23.37
USA	400,074	60,840	376,536**	1.75**
Algeria	126,806	†	2,219*	.13
Portugal	180,911	26*	231,475	26.15
Romania	171,717*	370**	168,388**	7.93**
South Africa	127,388	159**	63,588	2.38
West Germany	274,457	216,496	380,419	6.18
Yugoslavia	166,354	106*	161,149**	7.56**
Chile	161,837	1,110*	138,166	13.82
Greece	136,925	106*	94,127	10.46
Hungary	152,432	9,088*	98,249	9.25
All Other	418,309	515,697	6,205,289	†
World Total	7,635,383	1,086,413	7,510,796	†

*Estimate   † Not available   ** 1976 or latest available

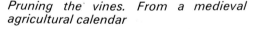

Pruning the vines. From a medieval agricultural calendar

HOW WINE IS MADE

There are several major classes of wine and thousands of variations within each class, but basically all wines have a common denominator in the way they are made: fermentation. This natural chemical process, in which man is really only the assistant, results in the conversion of plant sugar into equal parts of alcohol and carbon dioxide gas. A wide variety of fruits and vegetables can be fermented into wine but by far the best and most common source of wine is the grape.

In the fall of the year, grapes acquire two elements vital to the winemaking process: a sugar content of about 20%–25% and, on their skins, certain yeasts which can induce fermentation. The ripe grapes are quickly gathered from the vineyard and brought to the winery.

The simple machine which separates the grapes from the leaves and stems. The process is called 'égrappage', seen here in Bordeaux

There they are put through a simple machine that removes the leaves and stems and crushes the delicate grape skins. When the sugary juice flows out and makes contact with the skin yeasts, the winemaking process has begun.

Fermentation

The next steps depend upon which of the three basic types of wine the vintner intends to make: red, white or rosé. Color pigments in grapes are concentrated in the skin rather than the juice. If a vintner is going to make red wine, he must use dark-skinned grapes so that they can impart their color to the essentially clear juice. Thus, the first step in making red wines is simply to load all the material that emerges from the crusher — juice, skins, pulp and seeds — into large open vats. Here the yeasts can work to

Grapes going through extractors

change the sugar into alcohol, the carbon-dioxide can escape to the air and the clear juice can pick up color from the skins.

The procedure for making white wines begins in an essentially different way. Since the vintner wants to make a clear wine, he uses only the juice of the grape and not its solid parts. He can use either light or dark skinned grapes, but he must separate the juice from the rest of the grape before it picks up their stronger color and flavors. Therefore, the first step in white wine making is to press the grapes and to put only the resulting juice into the fermentation vat.

The procedure for starting rosé wines is a compromise between the methods described above. The vintner begins as he would with a red, that is, he uses at least some dark skinned grapes and includes their solids as well as juice in the fermentation vat. The difference is

Grapes fermenting in an open vat

that he removes these solids from the juice in the middle of fermentation, before they have given up all their color.

Fermentation can go on for hours or weeks depending upon the grapes used, environmental conditions and the style of wine the vintner seeks. Sooner or later, however, the process will come to a natural halt. This occurs when enough alcohol has been produced to numb the yeasts that sustain the conversion of sugar. At this point, the grape juice has turned into wine, but requires a series of finishing steps and the passage of time before it will become palatable. This second phase of the wine-making process is called cellaring.

Wine aging in a Bordeaux cellar

Cellaring

For red wine, the first step is to separate the liquid from the grape solids with which it has been fermented. About 80 per cent can be simply drained off and this 'free-run' wine or 'vin de goutte' is used for making the best quality wine. The remaining 20 per cent contains grape solids and must be separated by pressing. This 'vin de presse' is darker in color and stronger in taste and can be mixed to add force and volume to the 'vin de goutte' or it can be used to make a separate wine of lesser quality. The surviving grape solids can be given a second, hard pressing to produce a harsh wine called 'marc' that is distilled into brandy; but more often they are returned to the vineyard and spread along the rows as mulch and fertilizer.

All new wines, whether they are red, white or rosé must be protected from oxygen and from airborne bacteria which might turn them into vinegar. Usually, the young wine spends its first year in a large tank or barrel. During this period, several important events occur. First, there is a certain amount of evaporation and small quantities of the same wine must be regularly added to fill any air spaces. Second, the wine goes through another, much quieter, fermentation process in the spring of the year after the grapes were harvested. In this self-initiated process, the wine loses much of its ''green'' taste as its harsh malic acids are transformed into mild lactic acid.

Throughout the first year, minute particles in the wine are settling in the bottom of the barrel and must be separated to improve the clarity of the liquid. This is done by periodically siphoning off the wine into clean barrels, leaving a sediment or 'lees' behind. This procedure is called 'racking'. Traditionally it has been carried out when the wind was in the north, the weather was clear and the moon was full. This time-honored practice continues to the present day because it is under such conditions that atmospheric pressure is high and the 'lees' are therefore less likely to mix with the wine during racking. Barrel aging may go on for as much as three years and, in rare instances, even longer. During this time, the wine continues to be racked at intervals of several months. It gains in clarity, loses acidity and acquires more character from contact with the wood.

Lastly, the wine is clarified and stabilized to extend its life and brighten its appearance. One of the most ancient 'fining' procedures for wine is to add egg whites to the surface which, as they settle to the bottom, catch any remaining particles in the wine without changing its character. Other fining materials include gelatin and certain very fine types of clay. When the process is complete, the wine may be pumped through very fine filters to separate any residual yeasts or acids which might otherwise make the wine unstable. Finally, a trace of sulphite may be added to stop the growth of any micro-organisms.

Wines maturing in wooden casks before bottling, and stored in bottles in the background. The more modern stainless steel storage vats are shown below. Constant temperatures are essential in the cellaring process

Bottling

Bottling is a fairly straightforward procedure. The vintner's main concern is that his bottles be spotlessly clean so that nothing can spoil the wine after so much effort has gone into fermenting and cellaring. He also wants to ensure that the wine is exposed as little as possible to the atmosphere during bottling. Once in the bottle, a small space must be left to allow for expansion and contraction as the wine is exposed to temperature changes, but modern bottling machinery evacuates much of the oxygen in this space before the bottle is sealed. Wines can be shipped immediately after they are bottled, but most receive a period of rest before they leave the winery.

The modern bottling and packing process

The chemistry of bottle-aging is not thoroughly understood, but it is apparent that red wines mature quite differently from whites or rosés. The reason lies in the grape solids with which reds are fermented. In addition to color, the skins and seeds of red wine grapes contribute certain acids which, in combination with alcohol, act as the preservative which permits red wines to age for extended periods and to achieve an excellence rarely found in white or rosé wines. Some red wines will live as long as a man and they seem to have an almost human life cycle. Raw and ungainly in their youth, they become more finished and attractive with the passage of time. They eventually reach the peak of their powers and then go into a slow decline.

White wines contain much less preservative and with some notable exceptions, their principal charm lies in their youthful and refreshing properties. To enhance these qualities, fermentation of white wines usually is shorter than for reds, aging in wood seldom lasts more than 18 months and filtering is more stringent, but once in the bottle, little additional maturing is required. The same is true of rosé wines.

The Other Major Wine Types

These red, white and rosé wines can all be called 'natural' wines. Their alcoholic content may range from a low of about 9 per cent to a high of 15 per cent; their taste may vary from bone dry to syrupy sweet, but they are all the result of simple fermentation of fresh grapes and their character is entirely dependent upon the goodness of the grape and the skill of the vintner. Natural wines are the most common and diverse type of grape wines. They are usually served with meals.

But there are other wine types which, while beginning as natural products of fermentation, are altered by the addition of effervescence, alcohol or flavoring agents. Sparkling wines, the most famous example being Champagne, are made by adding grape sugar and yeast to already bottled natural wine. The carbon-dioxide which results is not permitted to escape and incorporates itself into the wine as bubbles of gas.

Fortified wines, which include sherry, port and vermouth, have grape brandy added (either before or after fermentation) which may raise their alcohol content to as much as 20 per cent. These are often called 'aperitif' or 'dessert' wines because they are most frequently drunk just before or after meals.

Flavored wines can combine elements of the three previous categories. They are usually made by adding herbs, spices or essences from fruits other than grapes. They may also be slightly carbonated or receive additional alcohol. German 'May Wine', Greek 'Restina' and U.S. 'Pop' wines are examples of this type.

More information about sparkling, fortified and flavored wines is given on pages 124-129.

CHAMPAGNE

Reims

Strasbourg

Paris

ALSACE

Colmar

VAL DE LOIRE

Angers

BOURGOGNE

Tours

Dijon

Nantes

JURA

La Rochelle

Macon

SAVOIE

COGNAC

Lyon

Cognac

CÔTES
DU
RHÔNE

BORDEAUX

Avignon

Bergerac

CÔTES
DE PROVENCE

Nice

Bordeaux

ARMAGNAC

Gaillac

Pau

Auch

LANGUEDOC

Marseille

JURANÇON

Perpignan

ROUSSILLON

The Story of Wine

PART II:

The Wines of Europe

THE WINES OF FRANCE

Foremost among the vinicultural nations of Europe – and the world – is France. Her wine production is enormous, but it is quality rather than quantity which has made French wines the standard by which all others are judged. This quality is largely the result of France's good fortune in having a wide variety of favorable growing conditions for cultivating and experimenting with the world's finest grape varieties. But it is also due to the French government and wine industry who have taken effective measures to protect their rich natural heritage in wine-making.

France began controlling the making and selling of wines nearly 200 years ago. There have always been unscrupulous vintners or wine merchants who will indulge in dishonest labelling or dilute good wines with poor ones (or even with water) but France was the first country to take practical steps to curb such practices. Over the years, the French laws have become increasingly strict and, although instances of fraud are still uncovered, the overall record is impressive. More effort goes into preserving the integrity of French wines than almost anything one can buy.

The modern system of controls over the production and marketing of French wines had its origins in the phylloxera epidemic of the 19th century. France's vineyards were left in a shambles and many growers tried to recoup their losses by planting other crops or by substituting higher yielding, but inferior grape varieties, often in unsuitable locations. Winemaking standards also declined with the result that the quality and competitiveness of French wines plummeted. The most grievous damage was done to the reputation of France's most famous vineyards.

When the prospect of economic failure joined with this threat to national pride, progressive wine growers solicited government support for more systematic control of the industry. They recognized that the future of French wines lay in quality rather than quantity and that this could be achieved only by maintaining the highest possible standards. They proceeded to define these standards for each area of production, based on the pre-phylloxera vineyard and winemaking practices, and sought laws to enforce these standards. But the government as a whole was hesitant to promulgate laws which would interfere with the freedom of the vintners to use their land or the wine merchants to run their businesses as they desired. Initial efforts to strengthen controls were met with lawsuits and public protests and, in some instances, the French army had to be called in to quell disorders.

Appellation Controlée Laws

Ultimately, it was the wine growers themselves who provided the impetus for the adoption of more stringent laws since many found that they could no longer make a living because of mistrust of their product. In 1935, the 'Appellation d'Origine Controlée' (controlled origin) laws were passed and in year succeeding year they have grown in scope, to the benefit of both wine makers and consumers. They now apply to all the best French vineyards, dictating what grapes may be grown, how they are to be planted, spaced, trellised, pruned, sprayed and picked. The laws specify the methods that may be used in fermenting, cellaring and finishing wines. Further, they limit the use of established vineyard names to the wines which are

The Château D'Issan belongs to the négociant family of Cruse. It is a 17th-century fortified manor within the complete moat of an old château-fort

actually produced in those areas and which meet the traditional standards for that type of wine.

The controlled origin laws have saved the French wine industry and led it to new heights of excellence. The wine public is pleased because it is getting dependable products of increasing quality while the wine industry benefits because renewed public confidence has increased demand and the price that the trade can ask. No one should assume, however, that the system is without flaws and that these laws guarantee that every bottle of French wine is a paragon of excellence. Stripped to its essentials, the laws simply ensure that vintners make as good a wine as they can from their land. Obviously, the quality of land varies greatly throughout the country and each year is marked by different weather. Laws can protect the consumer from malicious deceit in labelling, but they cannot alter the facts of nature.

Classes of French Wines

Basically, the law recognizes three broad classes of French wines. The most common and least expensive are produced under minimal government supervision and are referred to as 'Appellation Simple' wines. They can be made from virtually any sort of grape, grown under all sorts of conditions, and often contain wines imported from other countries (such as Algeria). These wines are rarely seen outside France.

The second major class of wines are those labeled 'Vins Délimites de Qualité Supérieure' (superior quality wines of limited production). The V.D.Q.S. wines, as they are usually called are grown from specified grapes in particular wine-growing areas. Their quality has been improving in recent years and, as the price of the finest French wines has risen, more and more V.D.Q.S. wines are being sold on the international market. The best represent very good value.

The top echelon of French wines, constituting the largest part of those marketed in the U.S., are those which bear the words 'Appellation Controlée' on their label. These are wines from the best vineyard regions and their production is strictly supervised to maintain the reputation of French viniculture. The standards for production are determined by an analysis of the climate, soil and terrain; the most suitable grape varieties, and the class and type of wines produced in the past. Progressively, higher standards are set for those localities where experience has demonstrated that unusually good wines can be made; more relaxed standards apply to broader, surrounding areas where conditions are less favorable. In ascending order of excellence, wines meeting Appellation Controlée standards are sold under the names of the region, district, village or individual vineyard in which they originate. For the consumer this means that the more specific the place name on the label, the more stringent have been the standards which the vintner has had to meet. It will usually be a better wine than one with the name of a larger area.

These qualitative distinctions between wines are sometimes blurred by extremes of weather and other external factors, but on the whole they serve their purpose very well. Anyone at all interested in French wines should know something about different regions and districts, and, if possible, about different vineyards and growers. The next sections are therefore devoted to sketching the essential 'geography' of those areas which produce the best French wines.

Bordeaux

The largest of the great wine regions of France is Bordeaux. Located in the southwest near the Atlantic Ocean, the terrain is relatively flat. It is crossed by two large rivers — the Dordogne and the Garonne — which meet north of the large port city of Bordeaux to form the Gironde estuary. Moderated by this great river system and the Atlantic ocean, the climate of the region is ideal for grape cultivation. The Bordeaux area is also blessed with a gravelly soil which permits good drainage and deep root penetration for the vines. It is these favorable circumstances which enables Bordeaux to produce not only more wine, but more great wine than any other region in France.

Much of this reputation rests on the fame of only five districts among the 22 that make up the Bordeaux wine region. The best among these is the Haut Médoc, whose four most famous townships — St. Estèphe, Pauillac, St. Julien and Margaux — encompass some of the most exalted vineyards in the world. To name but a few, they include Château Lafite-Rothschild, Château Mouton-Rothschild, Château Latour and Château Margaux.

The history of wine-making in Bordeaux is ancient. The Romans were using the Gironde estuary as a shipping port as early as the 1st century B.C., but there is no conclusive evidence that they were making wine in this area until the 4th century A.D. By that time the

A typically flat vineyard in the Haut Médoc, looking down to the Gironde estuary

Eleanor of Aquitaine and King Henry II of England

Roman Consul and poet Ausonius, who was a native of Bordeaux, was actively engaged in the wine trade and owned extensive vineyards which were probably located a few miles east of the port city.

After Roman rule ended in the 5th century, for a long period Bordeaux was raided by barbarians and pirates from the north and east. The wine trade declined and almost vanished, its revival dating only from the marriage of Eleanor of Aquitaine (the latter being the Roman name for this region) to King Henry of England in 1152. Under English rule, Bordeaux was protected from foreign depredations and was re-established as an important maritime and wine-growing center. Within a relatively brief period, England became the principal market for Bordeaux wines.

England retained possession of Bordeaux until 1453 when the commander of its forces, John Talbot, was killed at Castillon (not far from St. Emilion) in a battle won by the troops of the French King Charles VII, who earlier had been spurred by Joan of Arc to drive the English from French soil. However, this turn of events was greeted with little enthusiasm by the citizens of Bordeaux, whose vintners saw no advantage in French rule since their trade with England was easy and profitable. In fact, Bordeaux continued to supply wine to England, although it widened its trade by developing large markets in the Low Countries and Germany.

By the 16th century, French interest in the wines of Bordeaux was burgeoning and the vintners and merchants began organizing production and distribution in a more business-like way. The Médoc area was made into a center for large-scale viniculture by clearing forests and draining swamps at greater distances from Bordeaux. By the 17th century, members of the nobility and the rising merchant class had established some of the large wine estates we know today. Often these properties were graced with the small châteaux which originally were built as part-time residences and offices for the vineyard owners and have now become their trademarks.

The Bordeaux wine industry continued to expand until the Revolution of 1789. In its aftermath and during the Napoleonic period, many wine estates changed hands, but there was little of the destruction of property and fragmentation of ownership that occured in other areas of France. At the Restoration of the monarchy in 1815, the Bordeaux wine trade was relatively prosperous and by the middle of the 19th century the industry had begun to assume its present-day character as the most important vinicultural region of France in terms of output and rivalled only by the best vintages of Burgundy in terms of quality.

The Wines and The Grapes of Bordeaux

In a good year, Bordeaux produces about 70 million gallons of wine. A little over half of this was white but it is the red wines of Bordeaux which chiefly account for its fame. Most of the red wines are quite dry because the grapes from which they are made tend to be rich in tannin, the acid which makes wines tart in their youth but allows them to acquire smoothness and sophistication as they age. The principal grapes grown in the Bordeaux region are the cabernet sauvignon, cabernet franc, merlot, malbec and petit verdot.

Grapes from the best vineyards are given a long fermentation, sometimes as much as two weeks, so that the juice absorbs all the available color, tannin and flavor from the skins. The wine requires about two years of aging in wood before it is bottled and usually does not leave the winery until its third year. Although it is possible to drink a Bordeaux at this point, the better wines do not begin to show their true quality until

The vineyards of St. Emilion, one of the five great wine producing districts in Bordeaux

they are more than six years old. However, the lesser vineyards of Bordeaux usually ferment the grapes for a shorter period to produce lighter wines that require less aging before being consumed.

Both dry and sweet white wines are made in Bordeaux, but the principal grapes are the same for both; the sauvignon blanc and the semillon. The dry wines are made by picking the grapes during the normal harvest season when they have reached a sugar content of 20–25 per cent. During fermentation, virtually all of this sugar is converted into alcohol and the resulting wine is dry.

The best sweet wines of Bordeaux are made by leaving the grapes on the vines after the normal harvest time. The grapes, already high in sugar, are then attacked by a mold (Botrytis cinerea) which causes evaporation of the grape juice and thus increases the relative proportion of sugar. In this state, the grapes are described as having the 'pourriture noble' (noble rot); they behave differently during fermentation, because after sufficient alcohol has been generated to kill the yeasts that sustain fermentation, considerable sugar still remains. The very best of these sweet wines of Bordeaux are often regarded by experts as the peak of the wine-maker's art.

The wines of Bordeaux are basically blended wines. Even when they come from a single vineyard, they are usually a combination of two or more different grape varieties. The proportions vary from vineyard to vineyard so that wines which originate from neighboring properties may be quite different. These differences, of course, are in addition to those which are caused by the slight variations in soil, terrain and climate between adjoining vineyards.

Over the years, certain great Bordeaux châteaux have become associated with a particular style of wine. Some châteaux produce a wine which is fuller in taste and body, taking many years to mature; other châteaux emphasize lighter qualities, but still produce a wine with considerable underlying strength. It is important to understand that these subleties are the result of the vintner's skills as well as of natural factors.

Much of the wine produced by the 22 generally recognized wine districts of Bordeaux is 'vin ordinaire' which seldom appears on the world wine market. Five of these districts, however, produce wines of such superlative quality that their names are familiar to almost anyone who drinks wine, particularly since many countries have 'borrowed' these names for their own wines. These districts are the Haut Médoc, St. Emilion, Pomerol, Graves and Sauternes.

Grapes affected by the rot 'pourriture noble'

The vineyards of the Château Mouton Rothschild in the Médoc, where some of the rarest wines come from. They may be at their best after as much as twenty years' maturing. The vineyards shown here produce excellent claret

The Haut Médoc

The Médoc, a narrow strip of land along the left bank of the Garonne River and Gironde estuary north of the city of Bordeaux, is certainly the most famous red wine district of the Bordeaux. Along with the Côte de Nuits in Burgundy, it is probably the most prestigious in the world. Actually, there are two Médoc districts. The Haut (upper) Médoc is about 30 miles in length and lies up-river, closer to the city of Bordeaux. This is the district in which the region's greatest vineyards are concentrated. The Bas (lower) Médoc is about 20 miles long and lies downstream near the mouth of the Gironde. The vineyards here are less well situated and only a few have achieved recognition. Understandably, the vintners of this district are loath to underscore their relative inferiority by being known as 'Lower Médoc' and the Appellation Controlée laws in fact permit them to label their wines simply as 'Médoc'. This is a point to remember when buying a Haut Médoc wine.

Within the Haut Médoc district there are more than 20 villages or hamlets. Most of the vineyards produce wines which, under the standards set by the Appellation Controlée laws, go to market under district ('Haut Médoc') or regional ('Bordeaux') labels. Four villages, however, have vineyards which produce wines of significantly higher quality and are permitted to use the town name on their label. These four villages, from north to south, are St. Estèphe, Pauillac, St. Julien and Margaux. Furthermore, within each of these towns, there are certain vineyards whose quality is so outstanding that their wines are labeled with the vineyard name as well. This illustrates the basic principle of the French labeling system laid down in the Appellation Controlée laws: the more specific the label, the better the wine.

St. Estèphe

This most northerly of the famous villages of the Haut Médoc has a reputation for producing the sturdiest wines of the district. This stems from the fact that St. Estèphe borders the Bas Médoc and some of the heavy clay of that district spills over into the soil of St. Estèphe. Moreover, the vintners of St. Estèphe use a high proportion of cabernet sauvignon grapes which are the richest in flavor, darkest in color and heaviest in tannin (and therefore slowest maturing) of all the grapes used in the Haut Médoc. This tendency toward sturdiness is accented further by the common St. Estèphe practice of prolonged fermentation.

There are, of course, exceptions. Some vineyards have a high proportion of gravel and are planted in the lighter merlot grapes — and perhaps their vintners practice short fermentation. But, for the most part, it is fair to regard St. Estèphe as being the source of the Haut Médoc's 'hardest' wines; wines which are the most acid in their youth, but which have the strength to go on to a magnificent old age. They are, perhaps, less full in bouquet than the wines of the other three villages, but make up for this by their extraordinary richness of flavor.

St. Estèphe has fewer famous vineyards than Pauillac, St. Julien or Margaux. But it offers the largest selection of wines from excellent secondary vineyards, usually called 'crus bourgeois'. As such, St. Estèphe wines are worth watching for the many relatively unrecognized vineyards which produce wines of high quality and good value.

The list of St. Estèphe wines includes its most famous vineyards and its better crus bourgeois'. On a wine label, most of these vineyard names would be preceded by the word 'Château' or 'Château de'.

The Vineyards of St. Estèphe	
Beauséjour	Ladouys
Beau Site	Lafite-Carcasset
Calon-Segur	Lafon-Rochet
Canteloup	Leyssac
Capbern	MacCarthy
Clauzet	Marbuzet
Clos St. Estèphe	Meyney
Cos d'Estournel	Montrose
Cos Labory	Morin
Coutelin-Merville	Ormes de Pez
Crock	Pez
Cru Roche	Phélan-Segur
Fatin	Picard
Fontpetite	Plantier Rose
Grand	Pomys
Village-Capbern	Tour de Pez
Haye	Tour du Haut
Haut Marbuzet	Vignoble
Houissant	Tronquoy-Lalande

The cellars of a wine-merchant in Bordeaux

Pauillac

This town is almost universally regarded as the most important source of fine red wines in the Haut Médoc and, many would say, in the world. Its parade of famous vineyards is almost overwhelming, led by such legendary names as Château Lafite-Rothschild, Château Latour and Château Mouton-Rothschild.

The reasons for the excellence of Pauillac wines are not hard to find. First, the soil is the best sort of quick-draining, mineral-rich gravel and it is stacked in greater depth than anywhere else in the district. Second, the vineyards are unusually large and have enjoyed continuity of ownership for many years. As their fame and profits have increased, these estates have been able to re-invest in their vineyards and winery operations to produce a standard unsurpassed in the wine world. The result is a large number of wines which seem to combine all the best qualities of these from St. Estèphe, St. Julien and Margaux, yet still have an elegance and individuality of their own.

The proportion of different grape varieties used in making Pauillac wines varies from château to château. Among the most prestigious names, Lafite is perhaps the lightest and most refined because it uses a blend of approximately two-thirds cabernet sauvignon, one-sixth cabernet franc and one-sixth merlot. Latour is a heartier, more authoritative wine which contains as much as 80 per cent cabernet sauvignon. Mouton is the richest and slowest to mature because it is about 90 per cent cabernet sauvignon.

The Vineyards of Pauillac	
Anseillan	Haut Bages Averous
Balogues	Haut Bages Libéral
Haut-Bages	Haut Bages
Batailley	Monpelou
Bellegrave	Haut Batailley
Bellevue-	Haut Pauillac
Cordeillan-Bages	Lafite-Rothschild
Bellevue	Lafleur-Milon
St. Lambert	Latour
Clerc-Milon-	Lynch-Bages
Mondon	Lynch-Moussas
Colombier-	Liversan
Monpelou	Malécot
Couronne	Monpelou
Croizet-Bages	Mouton Baron
Cru Grand Duroc	Philippe
Pauillac	Mouton Cadet
Cru La Tour l'Aspic	Mouton-Rothschild
Daubot Haut-Bages	Pédesclaux
Duhart-Milon	Pibran
Duroc-Milon	Pichon-Lalande
Fonbadet	Pichon-Longueville
Grand Duroc-Milon	Pontet-Canet
Grand Puy-Ducasse	Tour Milon
Grand Puy-Lacoxte	Tour-Pibran

The Château Lafite, Pauillac. With two hundred acres it is one of the largest vineyards in the Médoc. It makes about 800 barrels of its very expensive wine, its second wine sells as Carruades de Château Lafite

The gravelly soil here is typical of the vineyards of Pauillac and St. Julien

St. Julien

This is the smallest of the four top vineyard villages of the Haut Médoc; it does not produce any wines which are classed with the most exalted vintages of Pauillac and Margaux and does not offer a large selection of fine secondary wines such as those found in St. Estèphe. Yet St. Julien has undisputed standing; its vineyards produce a range of consistently superior wines that have long been among the most popular from the Haut Médoc, perhaps because of their excellent quality for cost. Moreover, St. Julien wines share some of the elegance of the Pauillacs, the delicacy of Margaux, and the strength of St. Estèphes.

This happy blend of attributes is not difficult to explain. The soil of St. Julien is the same excellent gravel as in Pauillac, but has less depth. As a result, the St. Juliens tend to have less body than Pauillacs, but more than the Margaux, where the soil is shallower still. While St. Julien vintners use a high-proportion of cabernet sauvignon grapes fermentation is usually shorter than in St. Estèphe. Accordingly, the wines are high in tannin when young but assume a warm, smooth taste somewhat sooner. Again, there is danger in such generalizations and one can find St. Julien wines of widely different character, but it seems fair to think of its vineyards as producing some of the most appealing, friendly wines of the entire Haut Médoc.

The Vineyards of St. Julien

Belgrave	Lagrange
Beycheville	Langoa-Barton
Bontemps-Dubarry	Leoville-Barton
Branaire-Duluc-	Leoville-Lascases
Ducru	Leoville-Poyferre
Camensac	Moulin de la Rose
Domaine de	Moulin Riche
Trentaudon	St. Pierre-
Ducru-Beaucaillou	Bontemps
Glana	St. Pierre-Sevaistre
Gloria	Talbot
Gruaud-Larose	Tour Carnet

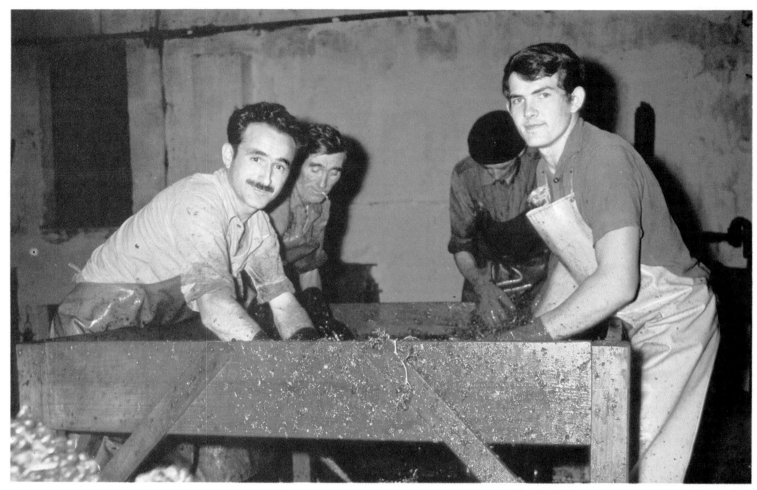

The process shown here in a Bordeaux vineyard is known as 'égrappage'. The grapes are separated from the leaves and stalks. This process can be seen on page 11 being done by machine, although is still frequently done by hand

Margaux

This village produces wines which, by comparison with the other three, are considered lighter and more refined. In Margaux, the gravel of the Haut Médoc becomes quite thin and the vines draw in fewer minerals, giving the wines less body and force. But in good years, a Margaux makes up for this with a delicacy and refinement that even the best Pauillacs find hard to match.

The outstanding vineyard of this village shares its name: Château Margaux. Long considered one of the four top properties of the district, it is always in great demand and fetches an extremely high price, which those who prize the unique perfume and subtle flavor of Château Margaux always seem to find worth paying. Like other Haut Médoc vineyards, the blending of different grape varieties at Château Margaux varies from year to year according to growing conditions. Typically, however, the combination is 50 per cent cabernet sauvignon, 35 per cent merlot, 10 per cent cabernet franc and 5 per cent petit verdot. These proportions, often followed by other Margaux vintners, are part of the secret behind the lightness of these wines.

The Vineyards of Margaux	
Abbé Gorsse de Gorsse	Kirwan
Abel Laurant	Labegorce
Alsème-Becker	Lagune
Angludet	Lamouroux
Boyd-Cantenac	Lascombes
Brane-Cantenac	Maléscot-St. Exupery
Cantemerle	Margaux
Cantenac-Brown	Marquis de Therme
Colonilla	Palmer
Dauzac	Pauquet
Desmirail	Paveil de Luze
Doumens	Pouget
Doubignon-Talbot	Prieure-Lichiné
Durfort-Vivens	Rausan-Segla
Ferriere	Rauzan-Gassies
Giscours	Ritz-Desmirail
Gurgue	Tertre
Issan	Tours du Mons

The 1855 Classification of the Haut Médoc

In the middle of the 19th century, in preparation for a major trade fair in Paris, a ranking was made of the best known wines of Bordeaux. This was chiefly comprised of the wines of Haut Médoc, but also included some from the Graves and Sauternes districts to the south. The majority of these classified wines are red and come from the four famous Haut Médoc villages.

This ranking, which has come to be known as the 1855 Classification, was made by the wine producers and merchants of Bordeaux, using nothing more elaborate than the price the wines had fetched in the trade over an extended period. Among red wines, they chose only 62 châteaux from several hundred well-regarded wine estates and ranked them in five qualitative groups. Today, some of the vineyards listed in 1855 might rate a different place on the list or might not be included at all, because, over the years some properties have deteriorated while others have improved. But, on the whole, the more than century-old ranking holds up rather well as a qualitative guide to the top châteaux of the Haut Médoc district; all these wines have the words 'Grand cru classé' on their labels.

In the following table the 1855 Classification is shown without the wines of Graves and Sauternes which are listed later.

Baskets full of harvested grapes

THE 1855 CLASSIFICATION OF RED BORDEAUX

Premiers Crus *(First Growths)*

Lafite	Pauillac
Margaux	Margaux
Latour	Pauillac

Deuxième Crus *(Second Growths)*

Mouton-Rothschild	Pauillac
Rausan-Ségla	Margaux
Rausan-Gassies	Margaux
Léoville-Las-Cases	St. Julien
Léoville-Poyferré	St. Julien
Léoville-Barton	St. Julien
Durfort-Vivens	Margaux
Lascombes	Margaux
Gruaud-Larose	St. Julien
Brane-Cantenac	Margaux
Pichon-Longueville	Pauillac
Pichon-Longueville-Lalande	Pauillac
Ducru-Beaucaillou	St. Julien
Cos-d'-Estournel	St. Estèphe
Montrose	St. Estèphe

Troisièmes Crus *(Third Growths)*

Kirwan	Margaux
Issan	Margaux
Lagrange	St. Julien
Langoa	St. Julien
Giscours	Margaux
Malescot-St.-Exupéry	Margaux
Cantenac-Brown	Margaux
Palmer	Margaux
La Lagune	Margaux
Desmirail	Margaux
Calon-Ségur	St. Estèphe
Ferrière	Margaux
Marquis d'Alesme-Becker	Margaux
Boyd-Cantenac	Margaux

Quatrièmes Crus *(Fourth Growths)*

St. Pierre-Sevaistre	St. Julien
St. Pierre-Bontemps	St. Julien
Branaire-Ducru	St. Julien
Talbot	St. Julien
Duhart-Milon	Pauillac
Pouget	Margaux
La Tour-Carnet	St. Julien
Lafon-Rochet	St. Estèphe
Beychevelle	St. Julien
Le Prieuré-Lichine	Margaux
Marquis-de-Terme	Margaux

Cinquièmes Crus *(Fifth Growths)*

Pontet-Canet	Pauillac
Batailley	Pauillac
Haut Batailley	Pauillac
Grand-Puy-Lacoste	Pauillac
Grand-Puy-Ducasse	Pauillac
Lynch-Bages	Pauillac
Lynch-Moussas	Pauillac
Dauzac	Margaux
Mouton-Baron-Philippe	Pauillac
Le Tertre	Margaux
Haut-Bages-Libéral	Pauillac
Pédesclaux	Pauillac
Belgrave	St. Julien
Camensac	St. Julien
Cos-Labory	St. Estèphe
Clerc-Milon-Mondon	Pauillac
Croizet-Bages	Pauillac
Cantemerle	Margaux

The 'Petits Châteaux' of the Haut Médoc

Ever since its publication, the 1855 Classification has been a widely-used shopping list for those who want to taste the best wines of Haut Médoc. More recently, it has become an investment guide for persons who are less interested in tasting wine than in making a profit from it. As a result, the price of many of the wines carried in the 1855 list has become grossly inflated. The intelligent wine buyer therefore should not confine his Haut Médoc purchases to these few most sought-after vineyards, but should look farther afield within this large and highly productive district.

For example, a good start might be the vineyard lists for each of the four famous Médoc villages (pages 23-26) which includes wines not in the 1855 Classification. Another alternative is the wine sold under village names which is produced by blending output from several lesser vineyards in these four villages. It can be even more rewarding, however, to choose wines from single vineyards among the other villages in the Haut Médoc district many of which produce relatively obscure, but highly creditable wines. Most fortunately situated among these other villages of the Haut Médoc are Labarde, Listrac, Ludon, Macau, Moulis and St. Laurent, but good vine-

yards and talented wine-makers are to be found in virtually every hamlet.

Most of the wines from these 'petits châteaux', beyond the borders of the four famed villages, go to market under their vineyard name, but are certified as nothing more than a district wine, e.g. 'Château de Lamarque, Appellation Haut-Médoc Controlée. This is a light, but good quality wine from a single vineyard. Its label indicates the name of the district, rather than the village in which the wine originated because the village does not have sufficient fine vineyards to be accorded appellation controlée status. Thus the Château de Lamarque and many other vineyards of

comparable quality tend to be dismissed merely as district blends by buyers pre-occupied with the 1855 Classification and the best-known names. Their oversight provides an opportunity for the wine-lover willing to search out the petits châteaux of the Haut Médoc.

To be candid, such wines have only occasionally been up to the high standard of the best known names – the Appellation Controlée authorities, after all, know their business. But many of the 'little wines' of the Haut Médoc are drawing closer to the quality level of the top growths. Until recently, wine-making was a largely intuitive and unscientific process and, at those fortunately situated vineyards which naturally produced good grapes, the lessons derived from experience were passed in private from one cellar-master to another. Vineyards on poorer land and vintners new to the trade had a hard time improving their wine. In the past few decades, however, there have been enormous advances in scientific understanding of wine-making and in the diffusion of that knowledge. The owner of a petit-château is now more likely to know what to do to overcome any deficiencies in his vineyard and winery and thus is able to come closer to the standards set by the great growths. Moreover, the radically increased world demand for wine – particularly from districts such as the Haut Médoc – has for the first time made it possible for small growers to prosper and to acquire the capital to improve their properties.

No doubt at some future date the number of Haut Médoc vineyards accorded Appellation Controllée status will be increased. Until then, however, the *petits châteaux* will provide a happy hunting ground for prudent wine buyers for, although these wines are advancing in quality, their prices have not yet risen as sharply as those vineyards included in the Classification of 1855.

The Château Loudenne in the Médoc

St. Emilion

Thirty miles east of Margaux, across the Garonne and Dordogne rivers, lie the other two principal red wine districts of Bordeaux: St. Emilion and Pomerol. To the novice, their wines seem much like those of the Haut Médoc. All three districts produce dry reds of uncommonly good quality which need considerable aging in the bottle before their real merit becomes apparent. The best are produced on relatively small properties with long histories and great reputations. The favor they enjoy on the world wine market makes them rather expensive and therefore wines for special occasions.

But to the experienced palate, there are substantial differences between the wines of these districts and those of Haut Médoc across the rivers. The contrast begins with the terrain of St. Emilion which, unlike the flat riverbank setting of the Haut Médoc, is situated in rolling countryside whose hilltops average about 300 feet. St. Emilion is also considerably smaller than the Haut Médoc, measuring only about six miles from east to west and three from north to south.

But the differences between St. Emilion and Haut Médoc also reach deep into the soil of the two areas. The soil of St. Emilion, which is richer than the gravel beds of the Haut Médoc, lies over a base of porous limestone that periodically gives way to patches of clay, silica, sand and chalk. This land provides an easier footing for grape vines but, as the vintners of the Haut Médoc argue, it also means that their fruit lacks the character that comes from a vine that has struggled for its existence.

The type of vines grown in St. Emilion are also different from Haut Médoc. The cabernet sauvignon is rarely found and the dominant varieties are the merlot, the malbec and the cabernet franc. These grapes grow more abundantly, permitting the vintners of St. Emilion to produce almost as much wine as the Haut Médoc, despite their smaller vineyard acreage. These grape varieties also ripen sooner which allows St. Emilion growers to get their harvest in before the late fall rains which sometimes damage the vineyards of the Haut Médoc. But there is a price to be paid for the greater productivity and convenience of cultivating the grapes of St. Emilion: compared to the cabernet sauvignon, they rarely yield a wine of the complexity and sophistication of the Haut Médoc.

The wines of St. Emilion, as well as those from the neighboring district of Pomerol, are often called 'the Burgundies of Bordeaux'. Although this is derogatory to the best Burgundies, (no experienced taster is likely to mistake them for wines from St. Emilion or Pomerol), it is true that the wines produced from merlot, malbec and cabernet franc grapes do have a similar style and life cycle. Compared to wines from cabernet sauvignon grapes, they offer a softer and more fruity bouquet, are smoother and less ascetic on the palate and do not live so long. In short, the wines of St. Emilion are more immediately appealing, but only those from the best vineyards are comparable to the wines from the major towns of the Haut Médoc.

The vineyards of St. Emilion may be divided into two parts. The larger and more ancient section is situated in the hills around the town of St. Emilion and the outlying hamlets of St. Christophe, St. Hippolyte and St. Laurant. The soil in this rolling terrain is a mixture of limestone, silica and chalk and the vineyards here are collectively referred to as the 'Côtes (hillside) St. Emilion'. The best know properties are Château Ausone (after the Roman consul and vintner Ausonious), Belair, Cannon, Gaffelière, Magdelaine, Pavie and the Clos Fourtet.

The other section of the St. Emilion district lies to the west where the land flattens and begins to slope down toward the Dordogne and its tributary, the Isle river. Here too, there is a significant change in the soil as the limestone base becomes mixed with patches of clay, sand and gravel. The vineyards of this section are known as the 'Graves (gravel) St. Emilion' and produce wines which are somewhat more full-bodied than those of the Côtes. The most famous properties are Châteaux Cheval Blanc, Corbin, Dominique, Figeac and Ripeau.

An official classification of the wines of St. Emilion was promulgated in 1955, a year in which many also hoped to see the Appellation Controlée authorities issue a revision of the century-old classification of the Haut Médoc. The St. Emilion ranking is less refined than its five-part predecessor, dividing the major vineyards into only two classes: 'Premiers Grands Crus' and 'Grands Crus'. Admittedly, the first class does acknowledge the historical, if not current, pre-eminence of Château Ausone and Château Cheval-Blanc, but the remaining 70 wines of both classes are simply listed in alphabetical order. This limits the utility of the classification as a qualitative guide but its design may prove to be intelligent if the list lasts as long as the Classification of 1855; in St. Emilion, as in the Médoc, vineyard qualities will vary with the talents and fortunes of their owners.

As in the Haut Médoc, there is increasing world demand for the classified growths of St. Emilion. However, the escalation in prices is not yet so dramatic, and therefore there is less pressure to seek out the *petits châteaux* of St. Emilion than those of the Haut Médoc. Nevertheless, it seems reasonable to assume that demand for the best known vineyards will continue to grow and that wine enthusiasts will begin to explore the less recognized producers of single vineyard wines as well as blends produced by cooperatives in the small villages of St. Emilion. Here, as in the Haut Médoc, new knowledge and money are raising production standards and an increasing number of good wines are becoming available at reasonable prices.

The Château Ausone. This land was originally cultivated as a vineyard by the Roman consul Ausonius ▶

The 1955 Classification of St. Emilion

Premiers Grands Crus Classés
Château Ausone
Château Cheval-Blanc
Château Beauséjour
Château Belair
Château Canon
Clos Fourtet
Château Figeac
Château La Gaffelière
Château Magdelaine
Château Pavie
Château Trottevieille

Grands Crus Classés
Château l'Angelus
Château L'Arrosée
Château Baleau
Château Balestard-la-Tonnelle
Château Bellevue
Château Berget
Château Cadet-Bon
Château Cadet-Piola
Château Canon-la-Gaffelière
Château Cap-de-Mourlin
Château Chapelle Madeleine
Château Chauvin
Château Corbin
Château Corbin-Michotte
Château Coutet

Château Clos-des-Jacobins
Château Croque-Michotte
Château Curé Bon
Château Dassault
Château Fonplégade
Château Fonroque
Château Franc Mayne
Château Grand-Barrail-Lamarzelle
Château Grand-Corbin-Figeac
Château Grand-Corbin Despagne
Château Grand-Corbin Pecresse
Château Grand Mayne
Château Grand Pontet
Château Grandes Murailles
Château Guadet-St-Julien
Château Haut-Corbin
Château Haut Sarpe
Château Jean Faure
Clos des Jacobins
Château La Carte
Château La Clotte
Château La Cluzière
Château La Couspaude
Château La Dominique
Clos La Madeleine
Château Larcis-Ducasse
Château Lamarzelle
Château Laniote

Château Larmande
Château Laroze
Château Lasserre
Château La-Tour-du-Pin-Figeac
Château La-Tour-Figeac
Château Le Châtelet
Château Le Couvent
Château Le Prieuré
Château Matras
Château Mauvezin
Château Moulin-du-Cadet
Clos de l'Oratoire
Château Pavie-Decesse
Château Pavie-Macquin
Château Pavillon-Cadet
Château Petit-Faurie-de-Souchard
Château Petit-Faurie-de-Soutard
Château Ripeau
Château Sansonnet
Château St-Georges-Côte-Pavie
Clos St-Martin
Château Soutard
Château Tertre-Daugay
Château Trimoulet
Château Trois Moulins
Château Troplong-Mondot
Château Villemaurine
Château Yon-Figeac

Pomerol

This small district lies to the west of St. Emilion and can be thought of as its western extension, sloping further down toward the Isle and Dordogne rivers and the port town of Libourne. The soil nearest the border of St. Emilion is the same mixture of clay, gravel and sand over a limestone base and it makes similarly full-bodied and highly aromatic wines. The grapes grown in Pomerol are also the same as in St. Emilion: merlot, malbec and cabernet franc. The typical vineyard is planted with about one-third of each variety, though the finest properties usually have a higher percentage of merlot.

Despite these common factors, the two districts have their separate identity. The wines of Pomerol, probably because of their lower elevation, are even more 'Burgundian' than those of St. Emilion; they tend to be darker in color, fruitier in bouquet, richer in flavor and heavier in body. They also mature a bit more quickly and fade a little sooner. Of all the Bordeaux reds, Pomerols probably offer the most immediate appeal, particularly, to those beginners who have not yet developed a taste for clarets from the cabernet sauvignon grape.

The history of wine-making in Pomerol also differs from that of St. Emilion. Although the district probably had vineyards in Roman times, it is doubtful that it was regarded as a distinct vinicultural area. Even a century ago, there are few references to Pomerol in the records of the Bordeaux wine trade. Pomerol is therefore the new-comer among the 'big five' districts, its wide popularity being established only since the dramatic expansion of the international wine market after World War II.

The average Pomerol vineyard is smaller than in St. Emilion and nowhere near as large as the major properties of the Haut Médoc. Their small output and relatively recent success means that few Pomerol vineyards are graced with any buildings that could legitimately be called a château; the average property has a modest stone farmhouse just large enough to accommodate the vintner's family and the winery.

Pomerol is also distinct in being the only one of the major districts whose vineyards have not been officially classified. There is general agreement that Château Pétrus is the outstanding property and it is often compared to the top growths of St. Emilion and the Haut Médoc. There are others nearly as good, however, and less inflated in price. The following unofficial list provides a guide to the most sought after Pomerols in the world market, followed by a group of less well-recognized but worthy vineyards. Following the example of St. Emilion, we have called the first group 'Premiers Grands Crus' and the second 'Grands Crus'.

POMEROL
Premiers Grands Crus
Pétrus

Clos l'Eglise
Conseillante
Eglise-Clinet
Evangile
Fleur
Fleur-Pétrus
Gay
Gazin
Latour-Pomerol
Nenin
Petit-Village
Trotanoy
Vieux Château Certan

Grands Crus
Beauregard
Bourgneuf
Cabanne
Caillou
Certain de May
Certan-Marzelle
Clinet
Clos du Clocher
Commanderie
Croix
Croix de Gay
Croix St. Georges
Cru de la Nouvelle Eglise
de la Gravette
de Sales
des Templiers
du Roy
Enclos
Feytit-Clinet
Gambaude-Gaillot
Grate-Cap
Grave-Trigant-de-Boisset
Guillot
Haut Maillet
Lagrange
Moulinet
Pignon de Gay
Plince
Pointe
Rene
Rouget
Taillefer

The vineyards of a château in the Pomerol ◀

Harvesting in the Pomerol vineyards ▶

Graves

The name Graves bespeaks the primary characteristic of its soil — gravel. It is probably the oldest wine district of Bordeaux, since it surrounds the port city from which, it is logical to assume, vineyards progressively expanded in ancient times. Graves is also one of the larger districts, beginning at the southern border of the Haut Médoc and running for about 30 miles up the left bank of the Garonne River where it encompasses the last of the five great wine districts: Sauternes.

In both soil and terrain, Graves is a continuation of the Haut Médoc, yet it does not afford so perfect a grape-growing environment. This is due largely to the fact that the district has not been so completely devoted to viniculture as the Haut Médoc. There the forests have been cleared, the swamps have been drained and the land reserved almost exclusively for vineyards. In Graves, some of the best grape growing areas have been displaced by towns and many vineyards are scattered in frost-prone patches between stands of pine trees and swamps. In this less than perfect setting, it is remarkable that the wines of Graves turn out to be as good as they are.

Until the rise of the Haut Médoc district, Graves was planted largely with red wine grapes, but today the city of Bordeaux has sprawled over much of the land best suited to these vines; only a few of the finest vineyards survive and now the production of the district is about one quarter red wine and three-quarters white. Much of the wine-buying public has come to think of the word Graves as a synonym for white Bordeaux, but many authorities maintain that the most distinguished growths are still the reds.

In Graves the primary red wine grape is the cabernet sauvignon, though the merlot and cabernet franc are also cultivated, making the Graves reds more like those of the Haut Médoc than any other district. They are difficult and full of tannin in their youth, but after about seven years from harvest they begin to smooth out into some of the most remarkably interesting wines found anywhere — including the Haut Médoc. There are important differences between the red wines of these two neighboring districts — some say that the Graves reds have a softer, silkier feel on the palate; others note a certain earthiness in the taste — but all agree that at their best, Graves wines rank with the finest growths of the Haut Médoc. This opinion was given official standing in 1855 when the most illustrious Graves red, Château Haut-Brion, was classified as a 'premier Crus' along with Lafite, Latour and Margaux of the Haut Médoc.

Today there are some who believe that Haut-Brion has slipped a bit or, at least, that some of its neighbors have risen to its lofty heights. But if this is so it was not reflected in the most recent classification of the Graves district made in 1959. The top 13 vineyards were presented in alphabetical order — with the exception of Haut Brion.

The white wines of Graves are made from varying combinations of the semillon and sauvignon blanc grapes, the former being dominant. Both dry and sweet versions are produced, but all the important growths are dry. As white wines go, those of Graves are assertive in their bouquet and taste. They seldom offer the charm of the Loire, the delicacy of the Rhine or the sophistication of the top Burgundy whites, but they can have an intriguing aroma, full flavor and solid body which entitles them to a place among the world's better white wines.

The following list shows those vineyards included in the official classification of 1959 which produce white Graves. Most of these properties also produce classified red growths (see red wine list); Laville Haut-Brion is the white wine of La Mission Haut-Brion. To this ranking it would be reasonable to add the white wine of Château Haut-Brion, but apparently it was not included at the owners' request.

The Red Wines of Graves

Haut-Brion

Bouscaut	La Tour Haut-Brion
Carbonnieux	La Tour Martillac
Domaine de	
Chevalier	Malartic-Lagravière
Fieuzal	Olivier
Haut-Bailly	Pape Clément
La Mission	
Haut-Brion	Smith-Haut-Lafite

The White Wines of Graves

Bouscaut
Carbonnieux
Couhins
Domaine de Chevalier
La Tour-Martillac
Laville Haut-Brion
Malartic-Lagravière
Olivier

The typically stony, gravelly soil in a Graves vineyard ▲
The stones retain heat after sunset ▶

Sauternes

This last of the five great districts produces wines unlike any others in France. Sauternes wines are the supreme white dessert wines of the world, rivalled only on occasion by the best growths of Germany. Unabashedly sweet, they offer an intensity of bouquet and lusciousness of flavor that must be sampled to be believed.

It is a sad fact, however, that in recent years Sauternes have been relatively unappreciated because the public has been following the maxim that for a wine to be good it must be dry. There can be little doubt that most appetizers and entrées are best complemented by drier wines. But for the dessert course or between meals, sweeter wines are ideal and it is a pity they are so often ignored.

It has not always been so. In the Bordeaux Classification of 1855, the quintessential Sauternes, Château Yquem, was ranked above all other wines including Lafite, Latour, Margaux and Haut-Brion. In the 19th century, Sauternes were the gifts of one royal family to another; the nobility of Tsarist Russia bought them in enormous quantity, and served them at every course of their grandest banquets.

With Sauternes wines out of fashion, some of the vintners of the district have fallen on hard times or have turned to other pursuits. A few have taken to making dry wines like those of Graves. The Appellation Controlée authorities have tried to discourage this practice, in the belief that it is a misuse of this specially endowed vinicultural district and that, sooner or later, classic Sauternes will once again be in great demand. Their tactic has been to prohibit the use of the name Sauternes for dry wines, thus forcing them to be sold as regional types (Bordeaux or Bordeaux Supérieur) which fetch a much lower price. There are signs that this has been a prudent policy, for the last few years have shown a decided upturn in the sales of traditional Sauternes. This is a logical development in view of the enormously increased demand for all French wines abroad and a growing sophistication on the part of the wine-buying public. Had the Appellation Controlée authorities not held fast, it is conceivable that many of the producers of these unique wines would have gone out of business before their audience returned.

Strictly speaking, the Sauternes district comprises those vineyards which lie south of the Ciron and west of the Garonne rivers within the boundaries of Graves. In practice, however, the neighboring district of Barsac, just north of the Ciron, is usually considered part of Sauternes because it specializes in the same sort of sweet wine. The vineyards of Barsac are permitted to use either their district name or that of Sauternes on their labels. The soil of both districts is essentially the same combination of gravel and sand as in Graves, but contains important traces of chalk. The grapes grown are also the same as in Graves, the semillon and sauvignon blanc, but some vineyards also cultivate some muscadelle vines. The method for making Sauternes wines requires late ripening and the presence of 'pourriture noble' (see page 13).

The following list presents the official classification of Sauternes wines made in 1855. Like the red wine vineyards of the Haut Médoc and Graves classified in the same year, several might now change position or possibly be displaced by another fine growth. On the whole, however, this classification provides a reasonably sound guide to the best wines of Sauternes and Barsac.

The stony ground of the vineyards in the Sauternes area

Premier Grand Cru	
Yquem	
Premiers Crus	
Climens	La Tour Blanche
Coutet	Rayne-Vigneau
Clos Haut	Rabaud-Promis
Payraguey	Rabaud-Sigalas
Guiraud	Rieussec
Lafaurie-Péyraguey	Suduiraut
Deuxièmes Crus	
Arche	Lamothe
Broustet	Malle
Caillou	Myrat
Doisy-Daëne	Nairac
Doisy-Vedrines	Romer
Filhot	Suau

An old French wine press, which is still being used

The Other Bordeaux Districts

The five most prominent districts discussed so far (Haut Médoc, with its four famous villages, St. Emilion, Pomerol, Graves and Sauternes) account for only about a quarter of the total output of Bordeaux wines. The other 17 districts (16 if Barsac is counted as part of Sauternes) produce wines which generally are of lesser quality but are still not without interest. Indeed, in this era of rapidly rising prices in the most famous districts and the diffusion of knowledge and capital to the less well-known districts, the wine enthusiast is well-advised to be familiar with other sources of Bordeaux wines.

Most of the vineyards in the minor districts traditionally have sold their wines in cask to the major shippers in Libourne or Bordeaux. There they are blended and bottled to be sold under the regional appellations 'Bordeaux' or 'Bordeaux Supérieur', the latter category simply denoting a minimum alcohol content of 10.5 per cent. Some of these shippers' wines may also bear the name of some fictitious château, but the regional appellation should alert the consumer to the fact that he is not being offered a single vineyard wine.

Increasingly, however, many of the small producers in these minor districts are selling their wines to local cooperatives, again to be blended and bottled, but to be sold under the appellation of their particular district. They can obtain a higher price for district (as opposed to regional) wines, and a small, but ever-growing number of vintners are estate-bottling single vineyard wines and selling them under district or even village appellations. What follows is a brief guide to the sorts of wines that are being marketed by the 'other' districts of Bordeaux.

On the left bank of the Gironde estuary and the Garonne River there are only two districts which have not yet been discussed in some detail. *Bas-Médoc* is a source of some good, if not excellent, dry reds. Occasional patches of gravelly soil permit a few exceptionally interesting wines, an example of which is Château Loudenne at St-Yzans. *Cérons* lies just north of Barsac and produces similar sweet whites at lower cost.

Between the Garonne and Dordogne rivers is a large area divided into seven vinicultural districts. The largest of these is the appropriately named Entre-Deux-Mers (between two seas) which produces about 90 per cent dry white wines and the balance in dry reds. The

Here in a wine cellar in Bordeaux the wine is stored at controlled temperatures in barrels. A shipping house buys wine from the château a few months old, and stores it until it is ready to ship or bottle

Vines in the Entre-Deux-Mers district

Premières Côtes de Bordeaux district faces Graves along the right bank of the Garonne and devotes 75 per cent of its output to white wines, more sweet than dry, and the remainder to reds. The small districts of *Loupiac, Ste. Croix du Mont* and *Ste Macaire* are opposite Barsac and Sauternes and their best products are sweet wines and a lesser number of dry whites. The most easterly district of the Bordeaux region is *Ste. Foy-Bordeaux* which produces a large quantity of rather heavy white wine and some strong, but rather undistinguished reds. The final district of this between-the-rivers area of Bordeaux is *Graves de Vayres.* Situated on the left bank of the Dordogne river across from Libourne, it specializes in dry whites, consciously imitating, but not equalling, the quality of Graves wines.

On the right bank of the Dordogne and the Gironde estuary, there are seven more districts whose production is almost entirely devoted to red wines. North of St. Emilion is a district comprised of several vineyard towns whose wines so resemble the lesser growths of St. Emilion that they are permitted to add the name of St. Emilion to their own. These towns are Lussac, Montagne, Parsac, Puisseguin, and St. Georges. Collectively they are known as the *Appellation St. Emilion* district. Just to the east are two small districts whose wines bear a similar affinity to those of Pomerol. These districts are called *Néac* and *Lalande de Pomerol.* Still further east are the districts of *Canon-Fronsac* and *Côtes de Fronsac.* Again, their wines are exclusively reds of above average quality among the wines of the minor districts.

The final two districts comprise an area as large as the Haut Médoc, which they face from the other side of the Gironde estuary. These are *Bourg* and *Blaye* which one prominent English writer refers to as 'the Cinderellas of Bordeaux'. The description is apt because, with increasing pressure on the more prominent districts, these two are suddenly being offered to the public as newly discovered princesses. Actually, Bourg and Blaye were making wine long before the Médoc vineyards were established and some of their wines are very good indeed. Red and white wines are made. Red are the more attractive.

Horse and cart in the Loire valley at harvest time

VAL DE LOIRE
Angers
Tour
Nantes
La Rochelle
COGNAC

THE LOIRE

The wine district of the Loire is situated about 180 miles north of Bordeaux and is named for the great river which extends eastward from the Atlantic deep into central France. Vineyards of sufficient consequence to be included in the Appellation Controlée system are found for nearly 300 miles along its banks. Obviously, in so long a distance, there are considerable variations in soil, topography and grape varieties. Most Loire wines are white although there are some notable reds and rosés as well.

The Loire Valley is often referred to as 'the garden of France' and its wines have a flowery yet refreshing quality which makes them unusually attractive. Several adjectives tell the story: gay, charming, young, graceful. With few exceptions, the Loire wines are most appealing in their youth and are at their best drunk with the lighter fare of spring and summer.

Although the region produces only a handful of wines which can compete in quality with those from France's most prestigious vineyards, they are not to be dismissed as little more than 'vin ordinaire'. On the contrary, the vintners of the Loire have long made wines of genuine distinction and during the past twenty years an increasing number have gained recognition on the international market.

Starting up-river from the Atlantic, the first important vineyard district is Sèvre-et-Maine. Here the melon or

The muscadet grape, which grows well in the Loire valley

muscadet grape is cultivated to produce a very agreeable, light and dry white wine, usually sold under the name 'Muscadet de Sèvre-et-Maine', or (of lesser quality) 'Muscadet'. A little further up-stream, one comes to the Côteaux de la Loire (côteau means riverbank) which also produces a good white from the muscadet grape. Both wines are favorites in France as an accompaniment to oysters and mussels, but are increasingly enjoyed abroad on all kinds of occasions because their price is reasonable.

The next district to the east is Anjou, a very large and diverse vineyard area which is divided into several important sub-districts. Before delving into their specialties, however, it is useful to know that the Anjou wines most frequently seen are rosés. The best are made from cabernet franc or cabernet sauvignon grapes ('Rosé de Cabernet'); wine made from lesser varieties is simply 'Rosé d'Anjou'.

In the Anjou part of the Côteaux de la Loire the chenin blanc grape is cultivated and is sometimes called the pineau de la Loire. These are used to make a slightly sweet, but refreshing white wine, the best of which comes from the town of Savennières. The Chenin blanc is also the predominant grape in the Côteaux du Layon, used to make an even sweeter wine, the best coming from the vineyards of Bonnezeaux and Chaume. Further to the east, in the Côteaux de l'Aubance and Côteaux du Loir, a somewhat drier (and relatively unknown) white is produced as well as a substantial quantity of pleasant rosé.

Saumur is the most easterly Anjou district and is best known for its sparkling wine, made in the same way as in the Champagne region. Although not of comparable quality, this sparkling wine can be a pleasant alternative to Champagne and is often reasonably priced. The Saumur area is a fascinating one because many of its houses and wineries are built in caves which honeycomb the bluffs along the Loire.

Touraine, the area surrounding the ancient city of Tours, is the next great wine district. Like Anjou, it produces several sorts of wines in a number of important sub-districts, but its most typical products are whites from the chenin blanc grape and rosés from the cabernet franc. The only reds of consequence in the Loire also come from Touraine, from the sub-districts of Chinon and Bourgeuil (and St. Nicholas de Bourgeuil). Too often, the growing season here is too short to make really impressive red wines, but at their best they can be very good. These reds (made from the cabernet franc grape) are rather light and soft and are said to have the scent of raspberries.

Surely the best known wines of Touraine, however, are the whites from Vouvray, which vary from year to year from dry to sweet according to the amount of sunshine. They are usually drunk before their third year to take advantage of their light, refreshing qualities, but the sweet wines made after a long hot summer should be kept longer. Sparkling whites similar to those of Saumur are also made in Vouvray.

The last important Loire vineyards are scattered among smaller districts beginning about 50 miles east of Tours. They specialize in dry whites, the best of which are made from the sauvignon blanc grape. Reuilly and Quincy wines have a hard finish and can be somewhat acid, but at their best are very good indeed. Sancerre's white is a distinguished wine with an aromatic bouquet and somewhat earthy taste. A good rosé made from pinot noir grapes is also found here.

From Pouilly come some of the most stylish whites in France. One needs to be careful with Pouilly wine labels, however. The best Pouilly is made from sauvignon blanc grapes grown in hillside vineyards and is labeled Pouilly-Fumé or sometimes Blanc-Fumé. It must not be confused with another white wine from the town of Pouilly-Fuissé in Burgundy. There is also a far less attractive wine, labeled Pouilly-sur-Loire, which is made from chasselas grapes grown in the clay soil along the riverbank.

Treading the grapes. A scene from the Bedford Hours, showing the occupations for September, French 1423

Entrance to the cellar at St. Nicholas de Bourgueil

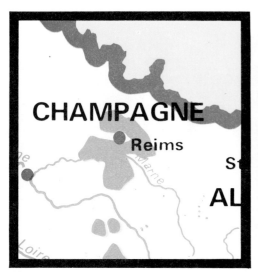

Champagne

Proceeding clockwise through France, the next great vinicultural region is Champagne. Situated some 85 miles northeast of Paris, this region is made up of three districts – Montagne de Rheims, Vallée de la Marne and the Côtes des Blancs. The first two are planted primarily with the dark-skinned pinot noir grape and the last with the white chardonnay variety. All but a fraction of these vineyards are devoted to the production of the world's finest sparkling white wines.

The name of Champagne has become so famous that it has been pirated by sparkling wine manufacturers the world over. Unfortunately, many of these producers have borrowed the name but not the technique of bottle-fermentation that was pioneered in Champagne and, to a large extent, accounts for the excellence of its wines. The 'méthode Champenoise' is a costly and time-consuming process and much of what is called 'Champagne' outside France is produced in large tanks, rather than bottles, or is simply made by pumping carbon-dioxide gas into natural wines. French law prohibits the use of the name Champagne for sparkling wines made by such methods, as it does for any sparkling wine made outside the Champagne region – even if the producer employs the 'méthode Champenoise'.

Champagne is produced in and around the cathedral city of Rheims by a number of long-established firms which buy their grapes from vineyards scattered through-

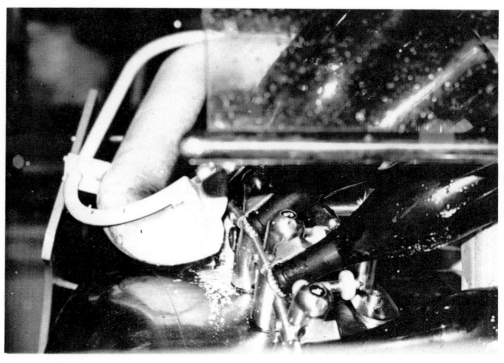

Above, the automatic 'dégorgement', or removal of sediment from the champagne. Below, the same process being done by hand

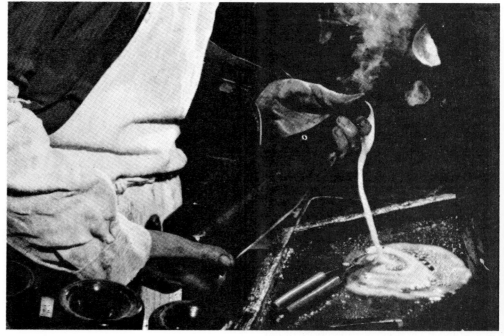

out the region's three districts. The process begins by making a dry, natural wine of high quality — usually from a combination of pinot noir and chardonnay grapes. Each of the Champagne houses makes its natural wines in an individual style which is reflected, ultimately, in the sparkling product; when only chardonnay grapes are used, the resulting wines are called 'blancs de blancs' (whites from whites).

The transformation into sparkling wine begins in the spring after their malolactic fermentation is complete. Sugar and yeast in the proportion of about 2 per cent by volume are then added to the new wine to induce yet another fermentation. Since the new fermentation produces enough carbon-dioxide gas to explode an ordinary bottle, the wine is tightly sealed in bottles which can withstand internal pressures of up to about 100 pounds per square inch. Usually the sugar and yeast have done their work within three months, but the newly effervescent wine is left undisturbed for about a year to insure that the yeast is exhausted and that the gas bubbles have incorporated themselves into the wine.

Then the difficult part of making bottle-fermented sparkling wine begins. The bottles are placed neck-down in racks and periodically turned to let the expired yeast cells and other residue accumulate at the base of the cork. This process is called 'remuage' and is done by highly skilled men who can turn many thousands of bottles in a single day. Many turns are required for each bottle, however, and a month or more may pass before all the solids have settled on the cork.

To remove the accumulated sediment, the wine is chilled to about 35°F. to reduce the explosive force of the carbon-dioxide gas. Then the neck of the bottle is chilled further to about 5°F. to trap the sediment in a plug of ice. When the cork is removed, there should be just enough pressure to expel this ice plug and so clear the wine. This delicate operation must be carried out with speed and precision to minimize the loss of the wine's hard-won effervescence.

If no sugar is added at this point and the bottle is immediately resealed, it will be labeled 'naturel'. Although these wines are preferred by some connoisseurs, they are too dry for most

Part of the automatic bottling process of champagne at the Château Cliquot

Giant stainless steel tanks for holding the still wine of Champagne

palates and constitute only a tiny fraction of total production. The vast majority are given a small dose of sugar — made into a syrup with a compatible white wine and a little brandy — before they are finally corked. The amount of sugar syrup or 'dosage' that is added can vary from about 1 per cent to 10 per cent. The driest style normally available is called 'Brut' and contains about 1 per cent sugar. The sweetness is slightly higher in bottles labeled 'Extra-sec' or 'Extra Dry' which have a sugar content of about 2 per cent, followed by those called 'Sec' or 'Dry' at 3 per cent. At the 5 per cent level are wines labeled 'Demi-Sec' or 'Semi-Dry' which are, in fact, distinctly sweet. Champagnes labeled 'Doux' or 'Sweet' contain about 10 per cent sugar and taste more of sugar than of wine. After the wine has received its 'dosage' and has been re-corked with a wire hood, it is returned to the cellars for additional aging. Champagne's slightly higher alcohol content (about 12%) and the presence of carbon-dioxide makes it one of the few white wines which responds well to extended periods in a bottle.

Champagne is at its best after five to ten years of aging, but only in exceptional years do the great houses of Champagne make a vintage wine and mark the year on their labels. These vintage champagnes are expensive and are not always better than the non-vintage champagnes which are a blend of several harvests, permitting the producer to maintain a consistent quality and house style whether the weather is favorable or not. The lack of a vintage date should cause the buyer little concern since most Champagnes are aged for five years before they are marketed and their popularity ensures that few non-vintage champagnes are unconsumed after ten years.

The unique thing about buying a bottle from Champagne is that, in a sense, one is buying a part of the winery. Since the law provides that all Champagne wines must be fermented in the bottle, the bottles are in effect, tiny fermentation vats. Sparkling wines which are made in other ways have always been a disappointment when compared to the classic procedure of the Champagne region. Today, the 'méthode champe-noise' is practiced by conscientious vintners in other parts of France and the world, but so far no one has succeeded in equaling the excellence of the original.

The cellars of Champagne. Some of these 'caves' are chalk pits, once used by the Romans. One firm uses trains in its 15 miles of tunnel

ALSACE

South-east of Champagne and not far from the German border is Alsace, a small region specializing in light-bodied, refreshing natural white wines noted for their particularly fragrant bouquet. Although the German grape varieties predominate, the wines of Alsace have an individuality of their own, and are of steadily improving quality, as evidenced by their recent inclusion in the Appellation Contrôlée system.

Alsace is a land of unusual beauty and its vineyards are among the most picturesque in all Europe – visitors can hardly realize that it has often been the scene of terrible wars. Generally speaking, Alsatian vineyards have flourished under French rule and suffered under the Germans who periodically have forced Alsatian vintners to concentrate on 'vin ordinaire' so that the German Rhine districts could be devoted exclusively to quality wines. Alsace continues to use a bottle whose shape is more German than French and names its wines after the variety of grapes from which they are made, in contrast to the usual French wine name system based on the region, district, village or vineyard of origin.

The vineyards of Alsace extend for about 50 miles from north to south along the eastern slope of the Vosges mountains which protect them from much of the cold, wet weather that would otherwise shorten the growing season. Colmar is the center of Alsace, but the famous vineyards are clustered around a

A view of Riquewihr   *Baskets full of freshly harvested grapes*

series of small villages that includes Guebwiller, Voegtlinshoffen, Ammerschwihr, Kayserberg, Riquewihr, Ribeauvillé and Bergheim.

Most of the vineyards are planted with white wine grapes, the most notable being the riesling and gewürztraminer. Lesser whites are produced from the chasselas, sylvanner and pinot blanc grapes. A significant amount of rosé wine (called Vin Gris) is also made in Alsace, but much of it is the result of blending inferior red and white wines. There is also a small quantity of good rosé made from the pinot noir grape and labeled Rosé d'Alsace.

Alsatian wines which bear such names as riesling or gewürztraminer are made exclusively from these grapes, while those that are a blend of wines from these noble' (edel) grapes are called Edelzwicker, or simply Zwicker if they are made from ordinary grapes. The alcoholic strength of Alsatian wines varies from about 10–13 per cent those having at least 11 per cent alcohol being permitted to use the words 'Grand Vin', 'Grand Cru' or 'Grand Reserve' on their labels.

Like the wines of the Loire, those of Alsace are made to be drunk young. Except for those rare years when a prolonged growing season permits the best grapes to gain extra amounts of sugar, Alsatian vintners do not try to make wines that require many years to reach maturity. Sweet smelling, but dry on the palate, Alsatian wines are compatible with a wide variety of dishes — a characteristic which is unusual in their German cousins.

The House of Hügel ▶
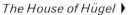

BURGUNDY

To the southwest of Alsace, between the great cities of Dijon and Lyon lies the only region that challenges Bordeaux in the variety and excellence of its wines — Burgundy. The vineyards of the former Duchy undeniably produce some of the finest and most famous wines of France. Certainly no other region of country has used its principal grapes, the pinot noir and the chardonnay, with such happy results.

Perhaps the most long-standing question in the wine world is whether Burgundy or Bordeaux is superior. Some argue that the wines of Burgundy are the kings of French viniculture and those of Bordeaux the queens. Others accept the royal imagery, but would reverse the descriptions. Some say that Burgundies are full of fire and humanity, while clarets (an old name for Bordeaux red wines) are cold and austere. Defenders of Bordeaux counter that Burgundy is a fine drink for neophytes, but that only experienced connoisseurs can appreciate the subtlety and sophistication of claret.

Whatever the merit of these arguments, there are important factual distinctions to bear in mind. In the first place, Burgundy's vineyards are only about one-third the size of those in Bordeaux. As a result Burgundies are

An old French wine press, now no longer used, but in a museum

usually more expensive than comparable Bordeaux wines because Burgundy's output is much smaller. Also, by an accident of history, the wines of Burgundy are made and sold quite differently.

At the time of the French Revolution, no wine region was more dominated by the Church than Burgundy. Like Bordeaux, the most important vineyards were relatively large, but they were owned more often by monasteries or churches than by individual landlords. These church lands became the object of revolutionary fury and were confiscated and turned over to the peasantry in small lots. In Bordeaux, the great wine châteaux were also seized, but they usually passed intact into the hands of the bourgeoisie.

This fragmentation of the Burgundy grape-growing lands has had lasting effects. First, since many vintners of differing skills and resources may share in what was once a single vineyard wines bearing the same vineyard name may differ substantially in quality. Second, the fragmention of production has made it more difficult for the French authorities to define and enforce standards as successfully as in Bordeaux. Third, relatively few properties are large enough to do their own cellaring and marketing, so the number of château or 'estate-bottled' wines is limited. Instead, most vineyard owners in Burgundy sell their young wine to firms located in the principal towns which handle its aging, blending, bottling and distribution.

Every other major wine region also has such merchants, usually referred to as 'négociants', but their role is usually restricted to dealing with the wines of minor vineyards to be sold under village, district or regional names. The distinctive feature of Burgundy's merchants, who are called négociants-élèveurs, is that they have a part in aging, blending and bottling the wines of the major as well as the minor vineyards. Thus, they have a far greater influence over the characteristic wines of their region than is the case elsewhere. This is why anyone who buys a major Burgundy wine should

Grand officers of the Confrérie des Chevaliers du Tastevin. Founded in 1933, this wine fraternity has branches in countries all over the world

pay as much attention to the reputation of the merchant or shipper as to the reputation of the vineyard.

There are, of course, exceptions. A few vineyards have been consolidated so that they are large enough to sustain their own cellars, while some of Burgundy's most exalted wines fetch such a high price that small-scale, estate-bottling is economic. Such wines will be labeled with the confusingly similar, but legally authorized, phrases: 'Mis au Domaine', 'Mise du Domaine', 'Mise en bouteilles par le propriétaire or 'Mise en bouteilles à la propriété' which, loosely translated, mean 'bottled at the vineyard.' Unfortunately, some négociants often label their non-estate-bottled wines with like-sounding, but meaningless phrases such as 'Domaines (followed by the négociant's name)', or 'Mise en bouteilles dans mes caves' (bottled in my cellars).

There are several other key phrases on Burgundy wine labels which need to be known. As with other wines subject to the Appellation Controlée laws, those of Burgundy are sold under place names. The best wines are given the name of the vineyard from which they originate and those which meet progressively lower standards are sold under village, district and regional names. Each of these broad categories (except that for village wines) are further sub-divided into qualitative groupings which are indicated on the label. First, the vineyard wines are usually broken into at least two classes, the 'grands crus' (great growths) and 'premiers crus' (premier growths). Second, the district wines may appear in as many as three grades, e.g., 'Beaujolais Villages', 'Beaujolais Supérieur' and simple 'Beaujolais'. Finally, there are three classifications of regional wines:

'Bourgogne' which may come from any vineyard or combination of vineyards throughout the area, but must be made from pinot noir or chardonnay grapes; 'Bourgogne Ordinaire' which has a lower alcohol content and may be made in part from gamay or aligoté grapes; and 'Bourgogne Passe Tout Grains' (two-thirds gamay and one-third pinot noir) or 'Bourgogne Aligoté' (largely aligoté with some chardonnay).

This labelling appears complicated but, once understood, it gives a much more explicit guide to buying wine than is available from most other wine-making countries. But some knowledge of geography is needed to back up the label information. By custom, Burgundy is divided into three northern districts (Chablis, Côte de Nuits and Côte de Beaune) and three southern (Côte Chalonnaise, Côte Mâconnaise and Beaujolais).

The Burgundy valley

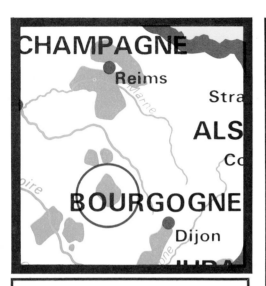

Chablis Grand Cru
Blanchots
Bougros
Grenouilles
La Moutonne
Les Clos
Les Preuses
Valmur
Vaudésir

Chablis Premier Cru
Beugnons
Boroy
Butteaux
Châpelots
Châtains
Côte de Fontenoy
Côte de Lechet
Forêts
Fourchaume
Lys
Mélinots
Monts de Milieu
Montée-de-Tonnerre
Mont-mains
Pied d'Aloup
Roncières
Séché
Trôeme
Vaillon
Vaucoupin
Vaugiraud
Vaulorent
Vaupulent
Vosgros

Chablis

The first of these northern districts, Chablis, has so famous a name that it has been appropriated by a host of countries to sell white wines resembling the original only in color.

Chablis is generally thought of as the driest of the world's best whites and is prized as an accompaniment to shellfish, particularly oysters. Its distinctive stony flavor comes from the chardonnay grape grown in chalky soil that is not found in other vineyard areas of Burgundy.

The Appellation Controlée laws recognize four grades of this wine: 'Chablis Grand Cru' which comes from the eight most famous vineyards and has an alcohol content of at least 11 per cent; 'Chablis Premier Cru' which comes from 24 other distinguished vineyards and has a minimum strength of 10.5 per cent alcohol; 'Chablis' from one of the many lesser vineyards and with at least 10 per cent alcohol; and 'Petit Chablis', which is a blend containing a guaranteed minimum of 9 per cent alcohol.

A 15th-century tapestry, now in the Cluny museum, Paris, shows the court visiting the vintners at harvest time

The Côte d'Or

The Côte de Nuits and Côte de Beaune, the second and third districts of northern Burgundy are often collectively referred to as the Côte d'Or (Slope of Gold). As this name implies, these districts yield the finest (and most expensive) wines. The vineyards are small, seldom more than a few acres each, and their modest appearance gives little hint of their quality. They are laid out in a strip about a half-mile wide which runs for 30 miles along the eastern slope of a low range of hills. This setting gives the vines good exposure to the morning sun and protects them from the westerly winds which can be bitter in so northerly a region. But the secret of the Côte d'Or probably lies less in its climate than in its soil. By most agricultural standards it is poor, but it happens to be extravagantly rich in the minerals required for growing the best wine grapes. From this thin strip of marvelously endowed land come some of the world's most elegant and admired wines – only in Bordeaux is there a comparable concentration of outstanding vineyards.

However, it is far more difficult to give authoritative guidance on the wines of the Côte de Nuits and Côte de Beaune than those of the Médoc. Since the middle of the 19th century, several classifications of the wines of the Côte d'Or have been developed, but none enjoys the wide-acceptance of the five-tiered ranking of the wines of Bordeaux made in 1855. The problem is the fragmentation of Burgundy's vineyards. In the Médoc, for example, Châteaux Lafite has but one proprietor: Baron Elie de Rothschild. His standards and skills apply to all 150 acres of vines on the estate and to every step of the wine-making process. Except for the vagaries of nature, a wine labeled Château Lafite-Rothschild will be a consistent quality and can be measured with some confidence against its competitors.

In contrast, in the Côte de Nuits vineyard of the Clos de Vougeot, 125 acres of vines are divided among some 60 owners. Their small parcels of land differ as much as their ambitions and talents, so that many different wines are made, all bearing the name Clos de Vougeot. For this reason, it is not easy to assign an overall rating to Clos de Vougeot and most other. Côte de Nuits vineyards nor to rank them against one another in any but the broadest terms.

Although the student of Burgundy wines will discover texts containing elaborate classifications of the Côte d'Or, most modern authorities confine themselves to a two-part ranking. They list as 'Grands Crus' those few vineyards which nearly everyone agrees represent the best in the district and which, over the years, have produced the most important wines. Then they follow with a second category, usually called 'Premiers Crus', which includes the lesser but still important vineyards which (in whole or in part) regularly produce distinguished wines. This two-fold classification is followed here.

Ancient wine amphorae from the museum in Beaune

The beautiful Château of Clos-Vougeot on the Côte d'Or at grape-harvesting time

The Côte de Nuits

This district comprises the northern half of the Slope of Gold and is Burgundy's pre-eminent source of red wines. Its northern exposure and special soil bring hardiness and strength to the wines, as well as a lushness of flavor and bouquet found in no other wines based on the pinot noir grape. The best of the Côte de Nuits are so rich in character that they deserve at least five years of aging before they are drunk. Although expensive, they can be memorable wines, especially if they have been cellared for a decade or more.

On this list the principal vineyards are ranked in alphabetical order under the names of the adjacent town or village. Nearly all towns have adopted the name of their most famous vineyard, though some have no grand crus within their borders. For example, the village of Gevrey has come to style itself 'Gevrey-Chambertin'. Some vineyards appear in two listings because they straddle a village border.

Vines at Vosne-Romanée on the Côte de Nuits. The reddish earth, rich in clay and lime produces some of the world's most expensive wines

RED WINE VINEYARDS OF THE CÔTE DE NUITS

FIXIN
Premiers Crus
Arvelots	Hervèlets
Cheusots	Meix-Bas
Clos du Chapitre	Perrière

GEVREY-CHAMBERTIN
Grands Crus
Chambertin
Chambertin-Clos de Bèze
Chapelle-Chambertin
Charmes-Chambertin
Gemaux-Chambertin
Griotte-Chambertin
Latricières-Chambertin
Mazis-Chambertin
Mazoyeres-Chambertin
Ruchottes-Chambertin
Premiers Crus
Bel Air	Craipillot
Cazetiers	Ergots
Champeux	Estournelles
Champonnets	Fonteny
Cherbaudes	Goulots
Closeau	Issarts
Clos du Chapitre	Lavaut
Clos St. Jacques	Perrière
Clos Prieur	Petite Chapelle
Combes Aux Moines	Poissenot
Combottes	Veroilles
Corbeaux	

MOREY-ST. DENIS
Grands Crus
Bonnes Mares	Clos St. Denis
Clos de la Roche	Clos de Tart
Premiers Crus
Bouchots	Faconnières
Calouères	Fremières
Chabiots	Froichots
Chaffots	Genevrières
Charmes	Gruencheres
Charrières	Maison Brûlée
Chénevery	Mauchamps
Clos Baulet	Meix-Rentiers
Clos Bussière	Millandes
Clos des Lambrays	Riotte
Clos des Ormes	Ruchots
Clos Sorbés	Sorbés
Côte Rôtie	

CHAMBOLLE-MUSIGNY
Grands Crus
Bonnes Mares	Musigny
Clos de Tart	
Premiers Crus
Amoureuses	Fousselottes
Baudes	Fuées
Beaux Bruns	Groseilles
Borniques	Gruenchers
Charmes	Haut Doix
Chatelots	Lavrottes
Combottes	Noirots
Cras	Plantes
Derriere La Grange	Sentiers

VOUGEOT
Grands Crus
Clos de Vougeot
Premiers Crus
Clos de la Perrière	Petits Vougeots

FLAGEZ-ECHÉZEAUX
Grands Crus
Echézeaux	Grands Echézeaux

*(often sells its wines under the name Vosne-Romanée)

VOSNE-ROMANÉE
Grands Crus
Richebourg	Romanée-St. Vivant
La Romanée	La Tache
La Romanée-Conti	
Premiers Crus
Beaux Monts	Grande Rue
Brûlées	Malconsorts
Chaumes	Petits Monts
Clos des Réas	Reignots
Gaudichots	Suchots

NUITS-ST. GEORGES
Premiers Crus
Aux Argillates	Perrière-Noblet
Aux Boudots	Porets
Aux Bousselots	Poulettes
Cailles	Procès
Chaboeufs	Pruliers
Chaignots	Richemone
Chaine-Carteau	Roncières
Champs Perdrix	Rue de Chaux
Château Gris	Saint Georges
Aux Cras	Aux Thorey
Aux Crots	Vallerots
Aux Damodes	Vaucrains
Aux Murgers	Vignes Rondes
Perrière	

PREMEAUX*
Premiers Crus
Clos des Argillières	Clos St. Marc
Clos Arlots	Corvées Paget
Clos des Corvées	Didiers
Clos des Forêts	Aux Perdrix
Clos de la Maréchale	

*(often sells its wines under the name of Nuits-St. Georges)

The vineyards which are not listed usually sell their wines to the négociants for blending. Mixed with other wines from the same town they will be sold under the name of that village. Blended with the wines of other villages, they will go to market under the district name. In addition to the important towns included in the above list, good blended wines may be sold under the names of lesser Côte de Nuits villages such as Brochon, Prissey, Comblanchien and Corgoloin. District wines are labeled simply Côte de Nuits or Côte de Nuits Villages.

As in Bordeaux, lesser known town and district wines can be good value for money. To keep vintners from exhausting their soil, the Appellation Controlée laws prohibit owners of Grand Cru vineyards from producing more than about 1,610 bottles per acre per year and Premier Cru vineyard owners from producing more than about 1,875 bottles per acre per year. In good years, despite wide spacing and rigid pruning, the vines can yield more than these amounts and the over-run is usually sold to the négociants-éléveurs to improve their town and district blends.

Some of the better known wine merchants of the Côte d'Or are presented in the list below. Their inclusion does not represent an endorsement, merely a sampling of those (among the 200 or more firms) which are most often seen on the international market. Each has its strengths in terms of access to individual vineyards and growers in the Côte d'Or; some specialize in the most renowned vineyard wines, while others trade primarily in town and district wines.

Bouchard Ainé
Bouchard Père et Fils
J. Calvet et Cie
Chanson Père et Fils
F. Chauvenet
Lupé Cholet et Cie
Jacque Dépagneux
Joseph Drouhin
J. Faiveley
Grivelet Père et Fils
Jaboulet-Verchere
Louis Jadot
Louis Latour
J. Mommesin
Albert Morot
J. Moreau
Rene Morey
de Moucheron
Patriarche Père et Fils
Piat Père et Fils
Pierre Ponnelle
Remaissenet, Père et Fils
Ropiteau Frères
Armand Rousseau
Sichel et Cie
Sichel et Fils Frères
Roland Thevenin
Jean Thorin
Charles Vienot
Comte George de Voguë

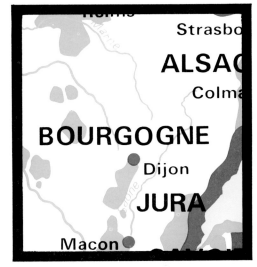

Côte de Beaune

Burgundy's third northern district, the Côte de Beaune, produces both red and white wines. The reds are made from the same pinot noir grape as in the Côte de Nuits, but a milder climate and less rich soil make them slightly softer and less full-bodied. As a result, some are ready to drink in under five years.

The fame of the white wines of the Côte de Beaune is so formidable that it often overshadows the reds. The whites are made from the same chardonnay grapes used in Chablis, but the limestone soil and easier climate of the Côte de Beaune gives them a more supple and luxurient character. The best white wines of this district are rivalled only by the best Chablis, the finest whites of Germany and few Sauternes.

In the following list of the Côte de Beaune's Grands and Premiers Crus vineyards the properties again are grouped by village. As in the Côte de Nuits, some villages attach the names of their most famous vineyards and some properties (the most famous being Montrachet) are associated with two villages.

The medieval French château of Saumur from the Très Riches Heures of the Duc de Berry. It was the most exquisite of all the prayer books of the Middle Ages, painted by Pol Limbourg and his brother about 1416. This extract shows the grape harvest in September

RED WINE VINEYARDS OF THE CÔTE DE BEAUNE

ALOXE-CORTON
Grands Crus
Corton	Corton-Languettes
Corton-Bressandes	Corton-Meix
Corton-Chaumes	Corton-Perrières
Corton-Clos du Roi	Corton-Pougets
Corton-Fietres	Corton-Rénardes
Corton-Grancey	Corton-Vigne du
Corton-Grèves	Saint

Premiers Crus
Chaillots	Meix
Fournières	en Pauland
Guerets	Valozières
Marechaudes	Vercots

BEAUNE
Premiers Crus
Aigrots	en Genet
Avaux	Grèves
Bas Teurons	sur les Grèves
Blanches Fleurs	Marconnets
Boucherottes	Mignotte
Bressandes	Montrevenots
Cent Vignes	en l'Orme
Champs Piments	Perrières
Chouacheux	Pertuisots
Clos des Mouches	Reversées
Clos de la Mousse	Seurey
Courcherais	Sizies
Cras	Teurons
Écu	Tielandry
Epenottes	Toussaints
Fèves	Vignes Franches

POMMARD
Premiers Crus
Argillières	Croix Noires
Arvelets	Derriere St. Jean
Boucherottes	Epenots
Chanlins Bas	Jarolières
Chanière	Petits Epenots
Chaponnières	Pezerolles
Les Charmats	Platiere
Clos Blanc	Poutures
Clos de la	Refene
Commaraine	Rugiens Bas
Clos Micot	Rugiens Haut
Clos du Verger	Sausilles
Combes Dessus	

VOLNAY
Premiers Crus
Angles	Clos des Chenes
Aussy	Fremiets
Barre	Lurets
Bousse d'Or	Mitans
Brouillard	Ormeau
Caillerets	Pitures Dessus
Carelles Dessous	Pointe d'Angles
Carelle sous la	Robardelle
Chapelle	Roncerets
Champans	Santenots
Chamlains	Taillepied
Clos Chevret	Village de Volnay

MEURSAULT*
Premiers Crus
Clos des Mouches
Santenots du
Dessus
*(most often sold as Volnay)

PULIGNY-MONTRACHET
Premier Cru
Le Cailleret

CHASSAGNE-MONTRACHET
Premiers Crus
Abbaye de Morgeot	Grand Clos
Boudriotte	Grands Ruchottes
Brusolles	Macherelles
Champs Gains	Maltroie
Chenevottes	Morgeot
Clos Pitois	Petit Clos
Clos St. Jean	Romanée
En Cailleret	Vergers

PERNAND-VERGELESSES*
Premiers Crus
Basse Vergelesses	Fichots
Caradeaux	Ile des Vergelesses
Creux de la Nette	

*(often sold under the name of
Aloxe-Corton)

SAVIGNY-LES-BEAUNE
Premiers Crus
Aux Vergelesses	Lavières
Basses Vergelesses	Marconnets
Charnières	Narbontons
Clous	Petit Godeaux
Fourneaux	Peuillets
Gravins	Redrescul
Guettes	Rouvrettes
Hauts Jarrons	Serpentières
Hauts Marconnets	Talmettes
Jarrons	

SANTENAY
Premiers Crus
Beauregard	Gravières
Beaurepaire	Maladière
Clos des Tavannes	Passe Temps
Comme	

WHITE WINE VINEYARDS OF THE COTE DE BEAUNE

ALOXE-CORTON
Grand Cru
Corton-Charlamagne
Premiers Crus
Pougets	Languettes

MEURSAULT
Premiers Crus
Barre	Jenelotte
Blagny	Limosin
Bouchere	Pelles
Casse-Tete	Perrières
Charmes	Petits Charrons
Chevalières	Petures
Cras	Piece sous le Bois
En Dos d'Ane	Poruzots
Genevrières	Poussots Dessous
Goute d'Or	Rougeots
Grands Charrons	Santenots
Gruyaches	Tessons

PULIGNY-MONTRACHET
Grands Crus
Chevalier-	Bienvenue-Bâtard-
Montrachet	Montrachet
Bâtard-Montrachet	Le Montrachet

Premiers Crus
Blagny	Garenne
Cailleret	Levrons
Chalumeaux	Meix
Champ Canet	Pucelles
Charmes	Referts
Clavoillon	Sous le Puits
Combettes	Truffière
Follatières	

CHASSAGNE-MONTRACHET
Grands Crus
Bâtard-Montrachet	Le Montrachet
Croits-Bâtard-	
Montrachet	

Premiers Crus
Cailleret	Ruchottes
Morgeot	

The lesser vineyards of the Côte de Beaune sell their wines to the négociants to be made into town or district blends. Most are sold under the names of the towns in the above listing, but may also bear the names of less famous villages like Ladoix-Serrigny, Chorey-les Beaune, Monthélie, Auxey-Duresses, Blagny, St. Aubin, Cheilly-les-Maranges, Dezize-les-Maranges and Sampigny-les-Maranges. The district wines are labeled Côte de Beaune or Côte de Beaune Villages. As in the Côte de Nuits, the town and district wines vary in quality according to the négociant-éléveur's access to sound wines from minor vineyards and the availability of over-runs from major wine properties.

Wine maturing in bottles in the cellars of the negotiant firm of Calvet, Beaune

The Côte de Beaune cannot be left without some attention to the town of Beaune and its extraordinary charity hospital. The town of Beaune is small by most standards — less than 20,000 souls — but it is the major urban center on the Côte d'Or and the wine capital of Burgundy. It has succeeded in preserving much of its medieval character and has a remarkable wine museum. Many of the best known négociants-éléveurs of Burgundy maintain their offices and cellars in Beaune, some of them within the ancient walls round the town.

It may seem odd that the most interesting wine history in Beaune is connected with its hospital, founded in 1443 and dedicated to the care of indigent and orphaned patients. The Hospices de Beaune continues to offer free health care to the poor and its prosperity is still based on its founder's belief that wealthy vineyard owners could improve their standing with the Almighty by bequeathing part of their best vineyards to the Hospices. Over the centuries, this unique institution has accumulated properties throughout the Côte de Beaune, the wines of which are sold each year to support the hospital's charitable work. The Hospices de Beaune auction takes place in late November and is a key event in the wine trade because the prices fetched for the hospital's wines usually set the standard for the rest of the Côte d'Or.

Most Hospices wines are sold under the name of the donor which can make the origin of the wines difficult to identify in modern terms. The following list shows the vineyards and towns of origin for each of the major wines which the Hospices produce.

◀The charity hospital in Beaune was founded in 1443 by Nicolas Rolin, Chancellor to Philip the Good, Duke of Burgundy, and now provides free medical care. The proceeds from the sale of the wine each year go towards providing the hospital with the most modern equipment

PRINCIPAL VINEYARDS OF THE HOSPICES DE BEAUNE

	Label Name	Vineyards	Town
RED:	Clos des Avaux	Avaux	Beaune
	Hugues & Louis Betault	Grèves & Aigrots	Beaune
	Billardet	Épenots & Noirons	Pommard
	Boillot	Duresses	Auxey-Duresses
	Blondeau	Champans & Taille-Pieds	Volnay
	Brunet	Bressandes & Mignotte	Beaune
	Dames de la Charité	Épenots & Rugiens	Pommard
	Dames Hospitalières	Bressandes & Mignotte	Beaune
	Maurice Drouhin	Avaux, Boucherottes, Champimonts & Grèves	Beaune
	Charlotte Dumay	Rénardes & Bressandes	Aloxe-Corton
	Estienne	Perrières & Bressandes	Beaune
	Fouquerand	Vergelesses & Gravains	Savigny-les-Beaune
	Forneret	Vergelesses & Gravains	Savigny-les-Beaune
	Gauvin	Santenots	Volnay
	Arthur Girard	Marconnets	Savigny-les-Beaune
	Rameau Lamarosse	Basses Vergelesses	Vergelesses
	Jacques Lebelin	Duresses	Monthélie
	Jehan de Massol	Santenots	Volnay
	General Muteau	Village & Carelle	Volnay
	Docteur Peste	Bressandes & Clos du Roi	Aloxe-Corton
	Nicolas Rolin	Cent-Vignes & Grèves	Beaune
	Rousseau-Deslandes	Cent-Vignes & Montrevenots	Beaune
	Guigone de Salins	Bressandes & Champimonts	Beaune
	Pierre Virely	Montée Rouge	Beaune
WHITE:	de Bahezre de Lanlay	Charmes	Meursault
	Baudot	Genevrières	Meursault
	Philippe le Bon	Genevrières	Meursault
	Goureau	Puruzots	Meursault
	Albert Grivault	Charmes	Meursault
	Jehan Humblot	Poruzots	Meursault
	Loppin	Criots	Meursault
	Francois de Salins	Charlemagne	Aloxe-Corton

The Côte Chalonnaise

This is the first of the three districts of southern Burgundy, where the climate, soil and terrain is generally less favorable than further north. But if the wines of southern Burgundy lack some quality and character, they are full of charm. Moreover they are produced in far greater quantities so their prices are much more reasonable.

The Côte Chalonnaise takes its name from the town of Chalon on the Sâone river. The vineyards situated on the river plain are of no real consequence, but those on the few patches of high ground (a southerly extension of the Slope of Gold) can produce noteworthy wines. The best vineyards generally face east or southeast, benefitting from the morning sun, and as in the Côte de Beaune, they are planted in pinot noir and chardonnay grapes. In addition to red and white natural wines, a large quantity of sparkling wine is produced in the Côte Chalonnaise.

Four villages of the Côte Chalonnaise have Appellation Controlée status and encompass some premier cru vineyards. From north to south, the first of these towns is Rully which is best known for its whites. The top vineyards are La Chaume, Chène, Gresigny, Margotty, Moulin à Vent, Rabource, Roclot and Sous Mont Palais. The wines have a good bouquet and bright flavor and are best drunk young.

Mercurey is almost exclusively a red wine town and certainly the best in this district. Its wines are lighter in character than those of the Côte de Beaune, but have a most attractive color and taste and can be drunk somewhat earlier. Mercurey wines are widely known and therefore tend to be more expensive than other Chalonnais reds; nevertheless, those from its ten premier cru vineyards still represent good value. These include Barraults, Byots Champmartins, Crets, Clos l'Evêque, Nogues, Tonnère, Vignes Blanches and Grand & Petit Voyens.

Givry, only five miles south of Mercurey, produces red wines which are usually more forceful, if not a little coarse. There are good premier cru vineyards in Givry, however, including Barande, Bois Chevaux, Cellier aux Moines, Champ Nallot, Clos St. Paul, Clos St. Pierre, Clos Salomon, Marolles and Survoisine.

At Montagny, the most southerly of the Côte Chalonnaise towns, the emphasis is on white wines. Although none of the individual vineyards are accorded Appellation Controlée status, the town wines can be very pleasant. Like the whites of Rully, they show good chardonnay character and are best drunk in their youth.

Harvesting in the Chalonnaise area ➤   *The beautiful valleys of Southern Burgundy*

Mount Solutré in the distinctive countryside of the Côte Mâconnaise

The Côte Mâconnaise

The second district of southern Burgundy is better known than the Côte Chalonnaise and encompasses a far larger area. It forms a rough triangle beginning near Tournus in the north, running southwest to the medieval monastic center at Cluny and continuing southeast to Mâcon, the town from which the district takes its name. The eastern border of the Côte Mâconnaise is the Sâone river.

The wines of this district are about equally divided between whites and reds, the former being by far the best. These are made largely from the chardonnay grape which benefits from the last great deposits of limestone soil in southern Burgundy. The red grape varieties are the pinot noir and gamay, but they are hampered because the climate is a bit too warm for the pinot grape and the soil is deficient in the granite on which gamay grapes thrive.

The finest vineyards of this district are concentrated in the southern corner of the triangle near Mâcon. Here the soil is especially rich in limestone on steep, quick-draining hillsides and the chardonnay grape produces wines which, if not the equal of the great Chablis and Côte de Beaune whites, are still among the most appealing of France. The vineyards are centered around the tiny villages of Pouilly and Fuissé whose combined name has become world famous. The Appellation Controlée laws permit the adjacent villages of Vergisson, Solutré and Chaintré also to sell their wines

View of the Mâcon region from the Northwest

under the name Pouilly-Fuissé. The best vineyards include Boutières, Brûlets, Chailloux, Chanrue, Château Fuissé, Châtenets, Le Clos, Clos de la Chapelle, Clos de Varambond, Menetrières, Peloux, Perrières, Pras, Versamières and Vignes-Blanches.

About one mile east lie the villages of Loché and Vinzelles which are permitted to precede their names with that of Pouilly. The best known vineyards include Château les Morandes, Château de la Vallée, Meziat and les Quarts, but their wines (made from the chardonnay grape) are usually regarded as less distinguished than those from Pouilly-Fuissé.

The rest of the white wines of the Côte Mâconnaise are usually sold in three classes under district names. The best are labeled Mâcon or Mâcon Supérieur followed by the name of one of the better-known vineyard towns, e.g. Mâcon Clessé or Mâcon Viré. These villages are situated on a ridge which runs north to south through the district. Those less well-known villages which share this high ground bottle their wines with the label Mâcon Villages. Finally, there are wines from less favorably situated vineyards which are simply labeled Mâcon. These contain less alcohol and are usually made with the pinot blanc grape as well as the chardonnay.

It should be noted that the wines of the Côte Mâconnaise are appearing increasingly under names other than the official appellations cited above. For example, much of the district's red wine is sold as the lowest class of Beaujolais, a practice which the government permits because of their essentially common characteristics and because the Beaujolais district alone cannot meet the world demand for this type of wine. Some white Mâconnais, usually pinot blanc from the lesser towns, goes to market as Beaujolais Blanc. In the U.S., where the public has become accustomed to buying wines named for the better grape varieties, a large amount of Mâconnais is now sold under the name Pinot Chardonnay.

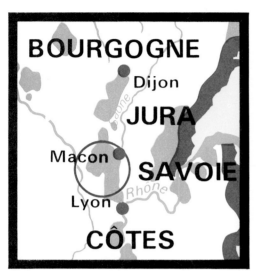

Beaujolais

This last district of southern Burgundy is certainly the best known and in the entire region only Chablis has a comparably famous name. Moreover, Beaujolais differs in so many ways from the rest of Burgundy that some believe it should not be counted as part of it. The average temperature is considerably higher and the soil turns from a limestone to a granite base; as a result, pinot and chardonnay grapes, common to all other Burgundy districts, are not grown in Beaujolais. The grape of the region is the gamay, a vine which was banished in 1395 from northern Burgundy by Philip the Bold as an 'evil and disloyal plant'.

Evil as it may be in the Côte d'Or, in Beaujolais the gamay grape makes a wine which is perhaps as widely drunk and appreciated as any in the world. It has a fresh, fruity bouquet, a winning taste and light body which make it the unequalled companion to everyday meals. Beaujolais is a wine for quaffing for the sheer fun of it and most is best drunk in its youth. The gamay grape is notably low in the acids which permit longevity in wine and this characteristic is emphasized by relatively short fermentation. As a result, most Beaujolais is ready to drink in one year and past its prime in three. Some wines – usually called Beaujolais Primeur – are even rushed to market within four months of the harvest. These infant wines epitomize the freshness of Beaujolais, but cannot show its full character.

The best wines of Beaujolais are sold under the names of nine villages grouped near the northern end of this 45-mile-long district. Here the terrain is hilly and particularly rich in granite, the vineyards are well drained and exposed to the sun. Certainly the most famous wine of the area is Moulin à Vent whose name has superseded that of the producing village, Romanèche-Thorins. But in many respects, Moulin à Vent is the least typical wine of Beaujolais. Here the gamay grape ripens particularly well and is given an unusually long fermentation. The result is a wine which begins to come into its own in its third year and may last for as much as a decade. The best known vineyard is Le Moulin à Vent, but others of note include Brainés, Carquelins, Champ de Cour, Maison Neuve, Pierre and Rouchauds.

Philip the Bold of Burgundy, who banished the gamay grape from North Burgundy in 1395.

Just to the north lie the villages of Chénas, Juliénas and St. Amour. Their vineyards yield wines which are more typical of Beaujolais as a whole but, like Moulin à Vent, are best if given a little time to age, two to three years being a good average. Continuing south, next come Fleurie and Chiroubles. The wines of Fleurie are a great favorite in the U.S., perhaps because the name is easily remembered and suggests the flowery quality of the wine's bouquet. Fleurie is a light wine, best in its first two years, while the wine from Chiroubles, although similar, is a little more robust.

The village of Morgon makes wines which are known for their earthiness and for lasting somewhat longer than most Beaujolais. A few miles further south stands a spectacular hill which marks the end of the district's most favored area. The vineyards on its slopes are known as the Côte de Brouilly and those around its base are simply called Brouilly. The Côte de Brouilly is regarded as the better of the two, but both Brouillys are much appreciated for their well-rounded character and above average alcohol content. They are best consumed within their first three years.

Next in quality after the wines from the nine best-known townships come those sold under the name Beaujolais Villages. These wines are made in the lesser vineyards of the villages already mentioned plus those of 26 surrounding villages where the growing conditions are nearly as good. Beaujolais Villages wines have been an excellent value because they were less in demand than the best-known Beaujolais. But the Appellation Controlée laws permit these villages to append their names to the Beaujolais Villages label. As a result, the best among them are gaining wider recognition.

The last two categories of wine made in this district are sold as 'Beaujolais Supérieur' and 'Beaujolais'. These may come from vineyards within any of the 59 other towns in the district. Most are located in southern Beaujolais and all are less well endowed in terms of soil, terrain and climate. Those wines sold as Beaujolais Supérieur must have at least 10 per cent alcohol content; simple Beaujolais need only contain 9 per cent. Nonetheless, the demand for these wines is high and production is often stretched by blending with the reds of the Côte Mâconnaise. Be wary of any sold without Appellation Controlée certification on the label as they may be blended with less compatible wines coming from beyond the Burgundy region and even from vineyards outside of France.

The vineyards at Fleurie, Beaujolais. The wine from Fleurie seems to have all the best qualities of this area

THE RHÔNE

The Rhône river flows west from Lake Geneva until it joins the Sâone at Lyon where Burgundy comes to an end. There the river turns south and begins an almost straight run for the Mediterranean — about 150 miles away. Scattered along its banks from Lyon to the sea are a number of well-known wine districts, known collectively as the Côtes du Rhône.

This is the most ancient wine region of France. The Greeks planted grapes near Marseilles as early as 600 B.C. and the Romans used the Rhône Valley as their gateway to the interior of France. At their fortified towns along the river, they established major vineyards that are still in use today. The residuum of Roman civilization and the strength of the Catholic Church kept the Rhône Valley the brightest section of France during the Dark and Medieval Ages. The civilized arts of language, music, poetry and wine-making were not only maintained, they flourished, reaching their apogee when the papacy was moved from Rome to Avignon during the years 1305–1370.

Since the rise of modern France, the Rhône region has become culturally less distinct and its wines have become over-shadowed by those of Burgundy and Bordeaux. As in those regions, the vineyards of the Rhône were laid low by phyloxera epidemic of the late 19th century and their wines were further debased by the fraudulent wine-making practices that followed. As a result of this experience, the vintners of the Rhône became the first champions of quality control and put into practice a predecessor of France's Appellation Controlée code. Today, although Rhône wines remain less well known than those of some other regions they are of higher quality than ever before and represent some of the best value among all French wines.

Rhône wines are often confused with those of Burgundy. Both areas produce large quantities of firm, full-bodied red wine and a lesser amount of fine whites. By tradition, the shape of the wine bottles used in the Rhône have been the same as those of Burgundy, and some restaurants, wine shops and books add to the confusion by grouping the wines of Burgundy with those of the Rhône.

But the contrasts between these two regions far outweigh the similarities. First, the environment is different; compared to Burgundy, the climate of the Rhône Valley can be described as harsh. During much of the grape growing season the heat can become almost tropical and at other times a fierce wind, the Mistral, whistles through the valley. The soil and terrain are also quite different, many of the vineyards being full of rocks and perched on steep hillsides above the river. The result is that none of the Burgundy grapes do well in the Rhône Valley and the vines that are planted have a rugged yet supple character that seems to be passed on to the wine.

Many adjectives have been used to describe the special characteristics of

From a 14th-century Book of Hours, French peasants working in the fields

The grape harvest in Vaucluse, in the Rhône Valley

Rhône wines — some of them derisive. The Burgundians, for example, call them 'sun-cooked' wines and are quick to point out that the region's most distinguished district, the Côte Rôtie, means 'the roasted slope'. Those more favorably disposed, however, can point to the remarkable longevity of Rhône wines, their robust body, alcoholic strength and engaging taste. Most will agree that Rhônes are the most virile wines of France, even if they are not the most sophisticated.

The principal grape of the Rhône is the syrah, which is supposed to have been introduced by Crusaders returning from the Middle East. A dozen other grapes are used, however, sharing with the syrah the need for intense heat for complete ripeness. Rhône vintners make no attempt to clear their land of rocks but instead spread them along the vineyard rows so that the sun's heat is reflected during the day and retained at night.

The Rhône is unusual among France's major wine regions in the extent to which several grapes are combined to make a single wine. By itself, the syrah yields too heavy a wine and benefits from blending with lighter varieties. Most Rhônes result from blending only two types of grape, but combinations involving many more are authorized by the Appellation Controlée laws. Blending not only makes the wines of the Rhône Valley more palatable and interesting than they would otherwise be, but also results in significant variations in character as one proceeds through the major districts.

A vineyard on the Rhône

The Côte Rôtie

This northernmost slope of the Rhône wine district is generally considered the most distinguished. It is located at a bend in the river near the town of Vienne and the vineyards are arranged on a series of terraces which run for two miles along the precipitous western bank of the Rhône. The lighter wines come from what is known as the Côte Blonde and the more earthy ones from the Côte Rhône, but in practice, most wines of the Côte Rôtie are a blend of the two.

The Appellation Controlée laws specify that the red wines of the Côte Rôtie be made 80 per cent from the syrah grape, the balance usually being completed by wine from the white viognier grape. The result is a velvety, full-bodied wine whose bouquet is said to evoke raspberries and truffles. While this may be argued, there is no disagreement about the quality of the wine and the 12,000 cases produced in an average year are hardly enough to meet world demand. Côte Rôtie wines are relatively long-lived and need at least four years in bottle to mature. The principal vineyards include Clapeyranne, Grand Vigne, Grande Plantée, Grosse Roche, Poyette and Turque.

Just south lie two small vineyard areas which produce Côte Rôtie whites. Condrieu consists of about 17 acres planted with the viognier grape which produces a white known for its big bouquet and earthy taste. Close by is Verin which encompasses the highly esteemed vineyard of Château Grillet. Its four acres of viognier vines enjoy an ideal southeastern exposure and the property is the smallest in France with its own Appellation Controlée designation. The wine is quite dry, very well-balanced and sophisticated in flavor.

The vineyards of the Hermitage. The syrah grape is one most often grown here, and the wines have the soft bouquet of honeysuckle

Hermitage

The Hermitage district lies about 40 miles south of Vienne, centered on the west bank town of Touron, but most of the best vineyards are on the east bank above the village of Tain-l'Hermitage. They are arranged on a dramatic hillside which has been used for growing grapes since Roman times. Today, the 350 acres of vineyards are divided between over 50 growers and produce about 60,000 gallons of wine a year, about two-thirds of which is red.

The reds of Hermitage are made chiefly from the syrah grape, but may contain up to 15 per cent of the marsanne or roussane varieties. Red Hermitage can be rough and bitter when it is young and needs more time to mature than other Rhône wines; five years is a good minimum for a fine Hermitage and the best can last for 50 years or more. The mature wine becomes surprisingly soft and rich and some say it has a bouquet of honey-suckle. As Hermitage ages, it should turn from the dark purple of its youth to a brownish cast which the French describe as 'onion skin'. The whites of Hermitage can also be impressive and are some of the longest lived of all white wines. Like the reds, they should not be opened too soon, but are usually drinkable in their fourth year.

The principal Hermitage vineyards include Bessarde, Chante Alouette, Chapelle, Croix, Ermite, Greffieux, L'Homme, Le Méal, Murets, Pierelle, and Signaux. Other key areas include Crozes-Hermitage, St. Joseph, Cornas and St. Péray. The vineyards of Crozes surround Hermitage and produce deep colored and robust reds similar to those of its neighbor, if a little less distinguished. St. Joseph and Cornas are west bank vineyards and the fact that they make their red wines entirely from syrah grapes may explain their relative lack of sophistication. St. Péray specializes in white wines (from the marsanne and roussane grapes).

Châteauneuf du Pape

This is by far the largest and best-known of the Rhône districts, usually producing more than a million gallons of good red wine each year. Châteauneuf gained its name from the 'new castle' which the popes of Avignon built on a hilltop overlooking the Rhône, but only a shell remains. The success of Châteauneuf wines in modern times is due largely to the efforts of Baron Le Roy de Boiseaumarie, whose efforts to enforce standards of quality wine-making in the 1930s became the model for the Appellation Controlée laws.

The wines from this area continue to be among the most closely regulated in production and marketing. The dominant grape is not the syrah but the grenache, and even more varieties (including the clairette, picpoule and terret) are used in blending. As a result, Châteauneuf wines are lighter than those of Côte Rôtie, faster to mature than Hermitage wines but remain incontestably a Rhône product in their purple hue, spicey bouquet and rich taste.

The wines of Châteauneuf have the highest minimum alcohol content of any French wine (12.5 per cent); most can be consumed in their third year since the grenache yields a wine which matures rather quickly. Accordingly, Châteauneuf does not last as long as the wines of the northern districts, but the very best will last for perhaps 20 years and show the same onion skin tone and soft bouquet of other Rhônes. Top properties include Château Fines Roches, Château Fortia, Château de la Nerthe, Clos de l'Oratoire des Papes, Gardine, Nallys, Saint-Patrice and Vaudrieu.

The Tavel vineyards produce excellent roses, on a limestone and chalk soil. Here the stoney ground is evident

The Château des Fines Roches, Châteauneuf-du-Pape. The rounded stones make an oven of the vineyard, keeping it hot long after sundown

Tavel

The wines of this district are perhaps more unexpected than they are important. Tavel devotes itself strictly to the production of rosés and in that limited category its wines are usually regarded as the best in France. The vineyards are located about five miles west of Châteauneuf du Pape in a soil based on limestone and chalk. The wine is made from the grenache grape and has a salmon-colored hue which distinguishes it from the pinker wines of lesser districts. It is one of the few rosés that can improve with a little age, chiefly because of its higher alcohol content, but it is best drunk young. Tavel is drier to the taste than most rosés and is particularly good with Mediterranean fish dishes. The best vineyards include Château Aqueria, Château de Clary and Tavel Cooperative.

THE WINES OF GERMANY

Perhaps the most extraordinary thing about the extraordinary wines of Germany is that they exist at all. The area in which they are produced is the most northerly of the world's major vinicultural regions, on a latitude with Newfoundland. Consequently, the summer growing season is short and sufficient sunshine to ripen the grapes is a perennial problem. Moreover, frost and freezing rains can maim the new growth of the vines in the spring or ruin a promising vintage before the grapes are harvested in the fall. In many years, the harvested grapes have insufficient sugar to make wine and beet or cane sugar must be added to sustain fermentation.

But the problems of making wine in Germany are not confined to the climate. To catch all the available sunlight, the best vineyards are planted on precipitous hillsides with some southern exposure. On these slopes the soil is a mixture of slate and clay so poor in nutrients that no crop other than wine grapes would survive. The maintenance of such vineyards is a herculean task. The soil keeps sliding down the mountainsides and must be carried up again on human backs. The slopes usually are too steep and the vineyard rows too narrow for animals and tractors.

Yet, from these unpropitious circumstances, the Germans draw some of the finest white wines on earth — light, delicious nectars that some experts consider wine-making's finest achievement. Somewhat sweet, their basic lightness makes them more versatile than Sauternes as table wines, but many Germans save their best vintages for use as an aperitif or to accompany a dessert.

The total output of German wines is relatively small, averaging between 150 and 200 million gallons per annum — only about one-tenth the production of France. It is fair to point out, however, that the average quality of German wines is certainly equal and probably superior to those of France. One reason for this high standard is that almost the entire wine industry (which as in France, is closely supervised by the government) concentrates on making a single type of wine from a limited number of grapes. The harsh environment prevents German vintners from making the wide variety of wines produced in other countries and, forced to be specialists, they pursue their work with characteristic determination and skill.

Nearly 90 per cent of the total output is in white wines with a flowery bouquet, delicately sweet flavor, limited body and low alcohol content. The few red wines that are made are produced from the spätburgunder (pinot noir) and portugeiser grapes but the short growing season usually prevents them from attaining the strength of aroma, taste and body normally expected in red wines.

Sloping vineyards near Bacharach
Vineyards at Ehrenfels, Germany, showing their steep slopes, terracing and difficult conditions

Wine Districts

The pre-eminent white wine grape is the riesling — sometimes referred to as the white or Johannisberger riesling — and all of Germany's finest wines are products of this grape. Like quality grapes the world over, they demand considerable care from the vintner and their yield is low. More prolific and easier to tend is the sylvaner, but its grapes produce a wine of less character and distinction than the riesling. These two major varieties have been repeatedly cross-bred to gain the advantages of both in a single grape. The most successful hybrid is named after its inventor, Muller-Thurgau, and is widely cultivated. Like most compromises, however, it is not completely satisfactory and this grape is not grown in Germany's best vineyards.

One other white wine grape deserves mention — the traminer. This variety and its well-known variant, the gewürztraminer, pose certain problems in cultivation, but they can yield an attractive wine distinguished from other German whites by its spicy bouquet.

The only wine-growing region of any consequence in Germany is the section of the Rhine River Valley between Bonn in the north and Basel in the south. There are a number of smaller rivers which flow into the Rhine on its journey through this region including the Ahr, Mosel, Nahe, Main and Neck. Their waters add to the Rhine's moderating effect on the climate of the region and their paths serve to define the principal vinicultural districts of the Rhine.

From north to south, the major wine districts are the Mosel, Rheingau, Rheinhessen, and Rheinpfalz. These are adjoined or interspersed by a number of lesser districts including the Ahr, Saar-Ruwer, Mittelrhein, Nahe, Franken, Würtemberg and Baden. Each of these districts contains a number of well-known wine towns and, in turn, many of the towns encompass certain vineyards of wide reputation.

Most German vineyards are extremely small by world standards, the average plot being only a few acres. Those vineyard owners who produce wines of high quality attempt to sell them as single vineyard products, a practice which accounts for the great number of German wine names. In general (see opposite), the labeling system employed in the Rhine Valley is similar to that of France — that is, most wines are named for the region, district, village or vineyard from which they originate.

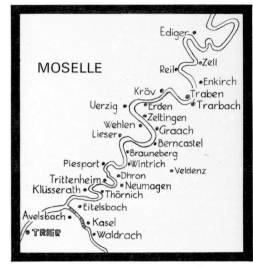

The Mosel (or Moselle)

This is the most northerly of the major districts and lies along the river of the same name which flows into Germany from France and Luxembourg, joining the Rhine at Koblenz. Along its 60-mile course, the Mosel is forced to turn repeatedly as it works its way through the mountainous terrain. The vineyards are situated on the rock faces above the river where they are protected from the cold winds by the valley's depth and serpentine configuration. The soil is almost pure, dark slate which captures the sun's warmth and permits rapid drainage for the vine roots. Every vineyard of consequence in this improbable, but exceptionally beautiful setting, is planted with the aristocratic riesling grape.

The Mosel vineyards begin south of Trier in the sub-district of Saar-Ruwer. Its name is derived from the two small rivers which flow into the Mosel from the south and provide more steep-sided, slate slopes for grape cultivation. Unfortunately they do not afford the same protection from cold as the Mosel itself and it is harder to ripen a crop. In favorable years, however, the Saar-Ruwer district yields some of Germany's most delicate and subtle whites.

The tall vines growing on the slate banks of the River Mosel are protected from the cold winds by the sheltered steepness of the banks, while the slate retains the sun's heat and drains water rapidly

The steep vineyards and terraces show clearly on the Mosel River bank.

The Vineyards of Mosel-Saar-Ruwer

Ayl: Kupp, Herrenberg
Eitelsbach: Karthauserhofberg
Kanzen: Sonnenberg, Altenberg
Kasel: Kohlenberg, Niesgen
Maximin Grünhaus: Bruderberg,
　Herrenberg
Oberemmel: Scharzberg, Hütte,
　Rosenberg
Ockfen: Bockstein, Geisberg,
　Herrenberg
Wiltingen: Schwarzhofberg,
　Klosterberg, Scharzberg

The principal wine villages and their finest vineyards are indicated in these tables.

Proceeding downstream and to the northeast, the next section of this district is called the Mittel-Mosel. Here the river becomes almost a canyon and better protection is afforded to the vineyards. The wines made along this part of Mosel are the finest of the district and among the very best of Germany. They have more strength than those of the Saar-Ruwer, but are still essentially light and delicate in character, often referred to as the queens of the Rhine wines.

The Vineyards of the Mittel-Mosel

Bernkastel: Doktor, Lay, Badstube,
Rosenberg, Schwanen.
Brauneberg: Juffer, Falkenberg.
Graach: Himmelreich, Domprobst.
Piesport: Goldtröpfchen, Lay,
Taubengarten.
Trittenheim: Laurentiusberg, Apotheke.
Ürzig: Würzgarten, Schwarzlay.
Wehlen: Sonnenuhr, Nonnenberg,
Klosterlay.
Zeltingen: Schlossberg, Sonnenuhr,
Himmelreich.

The Rheingau

This is the most celebrated of the Rhine districts, the equal in quality of Burgundy's Côte d'Or or Bordeaux's Haut Médoc. Its fame is largely due to its fortunate location on the south-facing slope of the Taunus range. These hills temporarily divert the Rhine from its northward course, forcing it into a broad westerly flow. The vine-covered slopes have maximum exposure to sunlight as well as the protection afforded by a large body of water which can moderate abrupt changes in the weather. Accordingly, the riesling grapes, with which the vineyards are exclusively planted, have an unequalled opportunity to ripen. Occasionally, they are even left on the vine well into the fall, when each additional day of sunlight increases the sugar and adds flavor.

The wines produced from these privileged vineyards have an intensity of bouquet and flavor which exceeds those from all the other districts. In comparison to most of the world's finest white wines, the Rheingaus are still fundamentally light and refined. But matched with their only rivals on the Rhine, the wines of the Mosel district, they appear gold rather than silver, perfumed rather than scented and masculine rather than feminine. They are, undisputedly, the Kings of the Rhine.

Assmanshausen is famous only for its red wine. The pinot noir grape grows well here

The Rheinhessen and Rheinpfalz

These two larger districts lie further to the south along the left bank of the Rhine. In both, the soil is richer, the terrain easier and the climate less severe than in the Mosel or the Rheingau. Perversely, the greatest wine grapes fail to respond to these more favorable conditions and the wines of these two districts have never achieved the same international recognition as their sisters to the north. Growers here cultivate less distinguished but more prolific grapes, like the sylvanner, muller-thurgau and traminer. However, it should be noted that there are some high quality vineyards in both Rheinhessen and Rheinpfalz and that the average wine from these two districts not only is very pleasant, it is less expensive.

The Vineyards of the Rheingau
Erbach: Marcobrunn, Siegelsberg, Steinmorgen.
Eltville: Sonnenberg, Langenstuck, Taubenberg.
Giesenheim: Rothenberg, Mauerchen, Katzenloch.
Hattenheim: Steinberg, Mannberg, Wisselbrunnen, Nussbrunnen.
Hochheim: Domdechaney, Kirchenstuck, Viktoria-Berg.
Johannisberg: Schloss Johannisberg, Klaus, Hölle.
Kiedrich: Graffenberg, Turmberg, Wasserrose.
Rauenthal: Baiken, Gehr, Wieshell, Wülfen.
Rüdesheim: Bergrottland, Berg Bronnen, Berg Lay.
Winkel: Schloss Vollrads, Hasensprung, Jesuitengarten.

The Vineyards of Rheinhessen and Rheinpfalz
Bingen: Scharlachberg, Ohligberg, Eisel.
Bodenheim: Kahlenberg, Hoch.
Deidesheim: Grainhübel, Hohenmorgan, Kieselberg.
Forst: Kirchenstuck, Jesuitengarten, Ungeheuer.
Kallstadt: Kobnert, Kreuz.
Königsbach: Idig, Satz.
Nackenheim: Engelsberg, Rothenberg, Steil.
Nierstein: Flachenhahl, Glock, Hipping, Rehbach, Orbel.
Oppenheim: Goldberg, Sacktrager, Kreuz.
Ruppertsberg: Kreuz, Gaisbohl, Hoheberg.
Wachenheim: Bohlig, Gerumpel, Goldbächel.

Only the most famous wine villages and vineyards are presented in these lists.

A simple crusher and stemmer stands by the vineyards which slope down to the River Rhine. The Rheinpfalz is the sunniest and driest part of Germany. The 150 villages in Rheinhessen grow wine as part or all of their livelihood

German Wine Labels

One of the minor ironies of the wine world is that wine buyers tend to be confused by German wine labels, even though no wine industry has made a greater effort to provide its customer with more explicit information. The system is really very simple and, once the buyer stops balking at all that Gothic script on the labels, he will discover that Rhine wines offer more truth in packaging than those of any other country.

The least important wines originate in the less well situated vineyards of any district and are usually made from high yield but undistinguished grapes. They are sold to wine merchants in the major villages for blending and bottling. These adequate but unexciting wines could go to market under regional or district names, but usually employ familiar trade names like Moselblümchen (Little Flower of the Mosel) or Liebfraumilch (Milk of the Virgin Mother).

At a somewhat higher level are the wines from vineyards planted with high quality grapes which are usually sold to a local village cooperative. There they are blended with others from the same village and grape variety and labeled accordingly; for example, a wine made entirely from riesling grapes grown in vineyards in the village of Johannisberg would be called 'Johannisberger Riesling'.

The finest Rhine wines are the product of high quality grapes, grown in a single vineyard in a specified year and made and bottled on that property by the owner. These wines are labeled with the name of the vineyard, usually following that of the village within which it is located. For example, the wine of the Klaus vineyard in Johannisberg would be called 'Johannisberger Klaus' and the label would usually indicate the grapes used, the year of their harvest and the fact that the wine was estate-bottled ('Eigene or Original Abfüllung'). The only exception involves the few most widely-recognized vineyards which are permitted to use their vineyard name alone, e.g. Steinberg, Scharzhofberg or Schloss Johannisberg, without explicitly indicating estate bottling, grape type (the riesling), or their town of origin.

A vineyard at Rüdesheim on the River Rhine. A large cooperative at Rüdesheim produces excellent blended wines

In 1971, the German government promulgated a new set of wine laws which have caused major changes in the industry. For example, to reduce the huge number of individual vineyard names — more than 30,000 had been officially recognized — the new laws required that any vineyard less than about 12 acres in size must adopt the name of one of its larger and more famous neighbors. The owners of the 10,000 or more small and obscure vineyards which were affected are almost sure to profit in the long run, but their outrage when the law erased the original names is easy to imagine.

The new wine laws are already helping the wine buyer, since under the new laws, the place names are more precisely defined, the types of grapes and their sugar content are more strictly regulated and ambiguous or misleading language is eliminated from wine labels. Wines produced under the new laws now constitute the great majority of German wines on retailers shelves and represent something of a victory for consumers.

The new laws also prescribe three qualitative classes for all German wines: 'Tafelwein' (table wine), 'Qualitätswein' (quality wine) and 'Qualitätswein mit Prädikat' (quality wine with certification). Tafelwein is Germany's 'vin ordinaire' and many of the regional or district blends automatically meet the minimal standards for this class. Basically, these consist of wines originating in any of the designated German wine districts (Gebiet) and made from any of the approved wine grapes. No minimum sugar content for the grapes is specified and it is assumed that many such wines will have to be heavily sugared to achieve an adequate alcohol content. The producers of these blended wines are prohibited from confusing the public by using the name of a single vineyard on the label. Although these wines now constitute the bulk of German production, few are expected to be sold outside the country.

Qualitätswein, which constitutes the bulk of the export trade, must meet more stringent requirements. These wines

The Mosel's greatest vineyards slope up the slate hills behind the town of Bern- kastel

must originate in a specific Gebiet (named on the label) and must be made from high quality grapes, also to be specified on the label. When harvested, these grapes must have enough natural sugar to make a wine with at least $8\frac{1}{2}$ per cent alcohol content. In practice, grapes with so little natural sugar always need extra sweetening, but the minimum natural sugar requirement serves to ensure that the grapes are ripe enough to impart their essential flavors to the wine. Finally, before a wine may be labeled Qualitätswein, it must be tested and tasted by a government panel and issued an official serial number. Wines which meet all of these standards may be district or village blends, or come from a single vineyard.

The Prädikat wines are the most strictly regulated, most limited in production and most sought after on the international wine market. They must originate in a recognized sub-district (Bereich) of a major Gebiet. In practice, they almost always come from one of the most favored group of vineyards (Gross-lage) or individual vineyards (Einsellage) within that Bereich and will also use this name on the label. These are the single vineyard wines with whose names the world has been familiar for many years; they must be made from the highest quality grapes (usually riesling) and, most important, must have a 10 per cent alcohol content without additional sugaring. This condition of the grapes is certified by the word 'Kabinett' on the label. Finally, 'Prädikat' wines must also pass a government review panel and be serially numbered.

In those frequent years when there is insufficient sunshine to ripen even the grapes in these best situated vineyards, their owners must add sugar to make their wines. Accordingly, these wines are required to appear on the market as a 'Qualitätswein', rather than as a 'Prädikat' wine. But in those growing seasons when the grapes not only meet the minimum Prädikat standards but become unusually rich in sugar, the labels carry an additional designation indicating exceptionally high quality.

Spätlese — grapes picked after the normal harvest with enough sugar to make a wine of about 10.5 per cent alcohol content.

Auslese — late-picked grapes, from which any unripe berries have been rejected, and which have enough sugar to make a wine of up to 12 per cent alcohol content.

Beerenauslese — very late-picked, individually selected berries which have enough sugar to make (theoretically) a wine of 16 per cent alcohol content. In practice, alcohol kills the yeasts which sustain fermentation as soon as it constitutes about 12 per cent of the wine. The unfermented sugar remains in the wine making beerenauslese wines exceptionally sweet.

Trockenbeerenauslese — extremely late-picked, individually selected berries which have been affected by 'edelfaule' (the same 'noble rot' as in Sauternes) and thus become so high in sugar that they could theoretically make a wine with an alcohol content of 20 per cent. These are the rarest, most intensely sweet and fabulously priced wines of the German wine industry.

A 17th-century oil painting of 'Peasants in the Tavern' by J. M. Molenaer.

Vineyards along the Rhine valley

The Italian countryside is covered with vines from the cool mountainous provinces in the north to the scorched southern islands of the Mediterranean. The output of these vineyards is prodigious, in recent years exceeding even that of France. The variety of Italian wine production is equally impressive; red, white, rosé, sparkling, fortified and flavored — the Italians make them all. This is the country the Greeks called Oenotria — the land of wine — and is also the country in which the viniculture of France and Germany has its roots.

Present day travellers to Italy still find that it produces some of the most appealing wines made anywhere. But, on returning home, they often discover that those vintages they found so charming in Rome or Florence or Asti are not available on their local merchants' shelves. Unlike France and Germany, which have energetically promoted the sale of their wines abroad, the Italians traditionally kept their best wines at home. When foreign shippers sought them out they were frustrated by the lack of organization and baffling vocabulary of the Italian wine industry. In contrast to its neighbors, Italy was slow legally to define the vinicultural geography of its countryside, identify the permissible grapes, regulate vineyard and winery practices and decide upon a standardized nomenclature for the many wine labels used in this most prolific of the wine nations.

Fortunately, this chaotic situation is now being brought under control. The

Vineyard in the Chianti region. The best Chianti is sold in Bordeaux bottles, not the well-known rafia-bound flask

Italian government has instituted a sound system for governing the nation's wine production along the same general lines as Germany and France. It starts from the same premise that effective regulation begins by defining wines in terms of their place of origin. Accordingly, the Italian wine code is called the Controlled Denomination of Origin (Denominazione di Origine Controllata or D.O.C.). It is administered by a joint government and wine industry council whose job is to define the wine regions of Italy, to determine the vines most suitable for the respective regions, districts, towns and vineyards, to establish rules for grape cultivation and wine-making and to specify the ter-

minology that may be used on labels bearing the D.O.C. seal.

The task has not been an easy one and, like their predecessors in France and Germany, the administrators of the D.O.C. are discovering that after nearly two decades of effort their work is not fully accomplished. Defining all wines in terms of their place of origin is extremely difficult when vintners have a commercial stake, as well as a personal pride, in retaining the traditional labels on their bottles, some of which carry place names borrowed from districts hundreds of miles from the producing vineyard.

Nevertheless, impressive gains have been made. The twenty ancient provinces of Italy have been accepted as the basic

vinicultural regions. Within these regions, many districts and sub-districts have been defined. Some of the wines which have traditionally been named for grape varieties, e.g. barbera or nebbiolo, have been modified by appending the area of production to the grape name, e.g. Barbera d'Asti or Nebbiolo d'Alba.

A system has also been devised for ranking all Italian wines in three qualitative groups, not unlike the system recently adopted in Germany. Italian 'vin ordinaire' is classified as 'Denominazione Semplice' — a designation which certifies only the region of a wine's origin, not the grapes used or the method of production. Higher quality wines are certified as 'Denominazione di Origine Controllata'

A wooden, hand-operated crusher and stemmer. This process is more often done by machinery

if they come from specified regions or districts, are made from certain grapes and conform to established production standards. They must be tested and tasted by a D.O.C. panel which must find them typical of the sort of wine traditionally produced in the place after which they are named. The best of Italian wines are given the designation 'Denominazione de Origine Controllata e Garantita' if they come from one of the famous districts or sub-districts and are made from the highest quality grapes according to the best vinicultural practices. These too must pass official analysis and sampling and, if successful, are labeled with a warranty of the Italian government.

Not every wine producer is happy with the changes in nomenclature and the government's attempt to supervise his work. Some have chosen not to participate in the system and have not applied for D.O.C. status. Their abstention, however, is short-sighted, for as consumers come to appreciate the improved quality and dependability of wines produced according to the new standards, they are likely to be less and less interested in wines without a D.O.C. label.

The list opposite sets forth those place names for wine which have so far been officially accepted for D.O.C. status. They are listed under the name of the region of which they form part. Outside Italy, nearly all wines found bearing these names belong to the intermediate category, since 'semplice' wines usually are not exported and the number of wines rated as 'garantita' is still limited.

Among these D.O.C. wines there are several which are of special interest because of their high quality or unusually attractive characteristics. For the most part, these better wines are red and come from the northern provinces.

Piedmont, in the northwest, is perhaps Italy's most richly endowed vinicultural region. Its most important district is Asti which lies between Turin and Genoa. This is the source of one of the world's best known sparkling whites – Asti Spumante. But the reds of this district are even more distinguished. These include Barolo, which some experts compare with the best of France's Côte Rôtie or Hermitage reds, and Barbaresco which is lighter and more often compared to a Bordeaux. Both of these wines are made with Italy's best red wine grape – the nebbiolo. Other well-regarded reds from the Piedmont district include the three Barberas. These are simpler, but most attractive and full-bodied wines made from the barbera grape. Finally, northeast of Turin, there is the famed sub-district of Gattinara. Its reds are paired with Barolo as Italy's finest and are made from the same nebbiolo vines.

Old wine-storing jars in an Italian museum

ITALIAN VINEYARDS GRANTED D.O.C. STATUS

Valle d'Aosta
Donnaz

Piemonte (Piedmont)
Asti Spumante
Barbera d'Alba
Barbera d'Asti
Barbera del Monferrato
Barbaresco
Barolo
Boca
Brachetto d'Acqui
Caluso Passito
Caluso Passito Liquoroso
Erbaluce di Caluso
Fara
Gattinara
Ghemme
Malvasia di Casorzo d'Asti
Moscato d'Asti Spumante
Moscato Naturale d'Asti
Nibbiolo d'Alba
Sizzano
Rubino di Cantavenna

Lombardia (Lombardy)
Botticino
Cellatica
Colli Morenici Montovani del Garda
Franciacorta Pinot
Franciacorta Rosso
Lugana
Oltrepis Pavese
Riviera del Garda
Tocai di S. Martino de-la Battaglia
Valtellina
Valtellina Superiore

Trentino-Alto Adige
Caldaro
Meranese di Collina
Santa Maddalena
Terlano
Teroldego Rotaliano

Friuli-Venezia Giulia
Colli Orientali del Friuli
Collio Georiziano
Grave del Friuli

Veneto (Venetia)
Bardolino
Bianco di Custoza
Breganze
Cabernet di Pramaggiore
Colli Euganei
Gambellara
Merlot di Pramaggiore
Prosecco di Conegliano-Valdobbiadene
Recioto della Valpolicella
Pecioto di Soave
Soave
Superiore di Cartizza
Tocai di Lison
Valpolicella
Valpolicella-Valpantena

Emilia-Romagna
Albana di Romagna
Gutterino dei Colli Piacentini
Lambrusco di Sorbara
Lambrusco Graspa Rossa di Castelvetro
Lambrusco Salomino di Santa Croce
Lambrusco Reggiano
Sangiovese di Romagna

Toscano (Tuscany)
Bianca di Pitigliano
Brunello di Montacino
Chianti
Chianti Classico
Chianti Colli Aretini
Chianti Colli Fiorentini
Chianti Colli Senesi
Chianti Colline Pisane
Chianti Montalbano
Chianti Rufina
Elba Bianco e Rosso
Montecarlo Bianco
Rosso delle Colline Lucchesi
Vermaccia di S. Gimignano
Vino Mobile di Montepulciano

Marche
Biancello del Metauro
Rosso Conero
Rosso Piceno
Verdicchio dei Castelli di Jesi
Verdicchio di Matelica
Vernaccia di Serrapetrona

Umbria
Orvieto
Torgiano Rosso e Bianco

Abruzzo
Montepulciano d'Abruzzo

Lazio (Latium)
Colli Albani
Colli Lanuvini Velletri
Cori
Est! Est! Est! di Montefiascone
Frascati
Marino
Merlot di Aprilia
Sangiovese di Aprilia
Trebbiano di Aprilia

Campania
Greco di Tufo
Ischia Bianco e Rosso
Ischia Bianco Superiore
Tuarsi

Puglia (Apulia)
Martina
Martina Franca
Locorotondo
San Servo Bianco, Rose, Rosso

Sicilia (Sicily)
Etna Bianco, Rose, Rosso
Marsala
Moscato Passito di Pantelleria

Sardegna (Sardinia)
Vernaccia di Oristano

A vineyard in Puglia, on the Gargano Peninsula

Venetia, in the northeast, has at least three wines of international reputation. Two of them are red and come from the sub-districts of Bardolino and Valpolicella, located just east of Lake Garda near Verona. These are light, engaging reds made from Corvina, negrara and molinara grapes and are at their best when less than three years old. For this reason and because of their fruity aroma and pleasant flavor, these wines are often called the Italian Beaujolais. To the east of Verona, the third notable wine of this region comes from the sub-district of Soave. By French standards, this dry white is somewhat coarse, but it is one of the most widely appreciated Italian whites.

In the north-central section of the country, Tuscany produces what is surely the most familiar name in Italian wine: Chianti. Until the D.O.C. laws came into effect virtually every corner of Italy produced a 'chianti', most of which damaged the reputation of the genuine wine which comes from the Tuscan hills near Florence. Of the eight names for Chianti now permitted under the law, the most distinguished is Chianti Classico. This designates the sub-district with the best-situated vineyards; their wines are marked with a neckband showing a black rooster in a red circle. Such fine chiantis are never sold in the familiar straw-wrapped bottles, but in Bordeaux-style bottles; the best are capable of maturing to a fine old age.

To the east of Tuscany lies the region of Marche which produces one of the most interesting Italian whites. This wine comes from the sub-district of Verdiccio dei Castelli di Jesi and is often sold in a variety of fancifully shaped bottles.

Finally, and far to the south in Sicily, there is Italy's most popular dessert wine: Marsala. Like a sherry, this wine begins as a rather dry white made from the cataratto, grillo or inzolia grapes. Then it is fortified with grape brandy to an alcoholic strength of about 18 per cent and sweetened with concentrated grape juice. Aged in wood for up to five years, it becomes quite dark in color and acquires a burnt sugar taste. Marsala comes in several qualitative grades and degrees of sweetness and is good not only as an aperitif but also as a flavoring in rich sauces.

THE OTHER WINES OF EUROPE

No slight is intended to the remaining wine countries of Europe by relegating them to a single chapter. Many of their wines are of very fine quality and, particularly when tasted where they are made, compare favorably with the better wines of the major vinicultural nations. However, at present relatively few of the wines of Switzerland, Austria, Hungary, Yugoslavia, Spain and Portugal are widely available on the international market, though they are likely to become more sought after as the prices of the famous wines of France and Germany continue to rise.

SWITZERLAND

The Swiss consume considerable quantities of wine, producing about 25 million gallons per year and importing an equal amount, largely from Burgundy. In fact, more Burgundy wines are imported by Switzerland than by any other country. The Swiss penchant for red Burgundy, particularly Beaujolais, is understandable on its own merits, but also stems from Burgundy's proximity and the fact that the bulk of Swiss wine is white.

The major Swiss vineyards are located around the lakes and rivers where there is protection from the cold. The most prominant regions are the Vaud, on the north shore of Lake Leman (Lake Geneva), and the Valais which stretches east of Lake Leman along the course of the Rhône River. These two regions make about 70 per cent of Swiss output; most of this wine is white and made from the chasselas grape.

The Vaud has two main districts, Lavaux and La Côte. Lavaux is considered the more distinguished and the important place names include Dézaley, Epesses, Lutry, St. Saphorin, Vevey and Villette. The principal district of the Valais region is Sion where white wines are made not only from the chasselas but also from the marsanne, pinot gris, and sylvaner grapes. This district also produces the best red wine of the Valais, from a mixture of pinot noir and gamay grapes, sold under the place name Dôle.

Other Swiss wine regions include the extensive vineyards on the north shore of Lake Neuchâtel near the French border, those just south of Germany around Baden and Lake Zurich, and the Ticino region which faces the Italian border near Lakes Maggiore and Lugano. The Neuchâtel region is best known for its light red wines from the pinot noir grape. Along the German border, most of the production is white wines of undistinguished quality. In the Ticino region, vintners produce both whites and reds, the reds made from the merlot grape being particularly successful.

A vineyard and the schloss in Switzerland. Almost every canton in Switzerland makes wine

AUSTRIA

Not surprisingly, the wines of Austria are largely in the German style; the majority are whites of varying degrees of sweetness, light in body and highly aromatic. The b st are made from the same grape as that of the Mosel and the Rheingau wines, which the Austrians have aptly dubbed the rheinriesling. The bulk of the good whites, however, are made from the veltliner grape and the finest examples display a clarity, spicey bouquet and crisp clean taste that can rival the rheinrieslings. Other less distinguished whites are made from the Italian riesling, muskat-ottonel and gewürztraminer.

All the important Austrian vineyards are concentrated in the east, including the two best-known regions around the cities of Krems and Vienna. In the region around Krems, known as Wachau, the vineyards face south on a range overlooking the Danube River. As in the best German districts, the vines grow in stony soil which has been painstakingly terraced to keep it from sliding down the hill. Most vineyards are planted in veltliner, but there are some superior rheinriesling vines as well.

The wine region around Vienna is divided into three districts. Just south of the city are the vineyards of Baden, producing both red and white wines. The whites are the favorites and are made from veltliner, sylvaner and gewürztraminer grapes. These wines are more pleasant than distinguished and most are never bottled, being drunk by the Viennese from barrel. One exception is the wine of Gumpoldskirchen which is often shipped abroad.

Southeast of Vienna, around Lake Neusiedler, is the large district of Burgenland. It produces both low quality reds from the pinot noir, and some very highly regarded sweet whites from German and Italian rieslings, as well as muskat-ottonel and gewürztraminer. North of Vienna there is another large district called Weinviertel. Here the veltliner produces wines which challenge those of the Wachau, offering a particularly attractive bouquet and refreshingly crisp taste.

Mountainous vineyards in Austria. Wine in Austria is often excellent straight from the barrel

HUNGARY

Unlike Austria, Hungary's vineyards spread from one end of the country to the other; the total output is more than twice that of Austria, including much more red wine. The most important wine districts range from west to east along the northern half of the country.

The first of these, and Hungary's most important source of fine table wines, lies along the northern shore of Lake Balaton. The best vineyards are planted in Italian riesling, furmint and keknyelu vines and high quality wines are usually labeled with the name of the grapes, e.g. Balatoni Riesling. These Balaton district whites taste strong and somewhat sweet to most foreigners, but they are the ideal accompaniment to many Hungarian dishes. To the north, the district of Barsonyos-Csaszar specializes in dry white wines.

East of the Danube, the first district of consequence is that of Matraalja. Its chief wine town is Eger, the source of Egri Bikaver (Bull's Blood) which is certainly the Hungarian red wine most often encountered abroad. Eger's vineyards also grow the merlot grape to produce a wine which is rather presumptuously labeled 'Médoc' and a light wine is made under the grape name Leanyka.

The wine most prized inside and outside Hungary is Tokay. These are sweet whites and at their best are in a class with the finest Rhines and Sauternes. They are made from furmint and harslevelu grapes which, in the most favorable years, are kept on the vines until they are attacked by the 'noble rot'. In Hungary the term for this condition is called 'aszu' and the fully sweet, dessert style tokays are labeled Tokaji Aszu. A less honeyed version is called Tokaji Szamorodni.

Harvesting in the Hungarian vineyards

YUGOSLAVIA

Yugoslavia produces about as much wine as Austria and Hungary combined and like its Italian neighbor to the west, makes wines of every description. In recent years, more and more Yugoslav wines have been exported and in quality for price they have proved to be unusually attractive.

The major Yugoslav wine regions are in the north, along the borders of Austria and Hungary, and in the west, facing the Adriatic Sea. In the center of the country, the land is too mountainous for viniculture and in the south and east, while a great deal of wine is produced, it is seldom of high quality.

The principal northern regions are Slovenia and Croatia. In Slovenia, the Ljutomer district produces some notable dry white wines. Foremost among these are the Laski and Rajnski Rizlings, produced from the Italian riesling grape which is known in Yugoslavia as the grasvina. Other good whites are the Traminec, from the gewürztraminer vine, and the Sipon, from furmint grapes. Croatia makes its own versions of the same wines plus a few others from pinot blanc, semillon, sauvignon blanc and muskat-ottonel varieties.

Along the Dalmatian coast, the emphasis shifts to reds and roses which vary in character from dark red to the

Grapes from the vineyards on the island of Korcula, one of the many wine growing islands off the Dalmatian coast of Yugoslavia. Yugoslavia produces about as much wine as Austria and Hungary combined. The main regions are Slovenia and Croatia

palest pink. The familiar cabernet and merlot grapes are used, as well as the native plavac and dingac, to make good quality red wines which are marketed under these grape names. Among the rosés, Opol is probably the most widely exported and is a pleasant wine.

SPAIN

Without any question, the premier wine of Spain is sherry — a name probably derived from repeated English mispronunciation of the district from which it comes — Jerez. Located deep in the south, on the Atlantic coast, the climate is dry and the soil is a chalk found only in two other great wine regions: Chablis and Champagne. The grapes which make the white wine on which sherry is based are the palomino and pedro ximinez. These factors of climate, soil and grape variety are vital, but the real secret of sherry is what is done after the grapes are picked.

First the bunches of grapes are spread on straw mats in the sun and dusted with some of the chalky albariza soil. This tends to intensify their flavor and improve their acidity. The wine is fermented until it is bone dry and then it is placed in white oak casks. At this point for virtually any other wine the vintner makes every effort to protect his wine from the air. But the sherry casks are left partially open for about three months to encourage the growth of an airborne yeast native to Jerez. For reasons not completely understood, this yeast seems to grow vigorously on the surface of some wines while ignoring others in the immediate area. Those sherries on which the yeast flourishes, making a surface crust called 'flor', become steadily drier and more interesting in flavor and are called 'finos'; those on which the flor does not develop are called 'olorosos' and are subsequently flavored and colored by the addition of sweet wine and grape concentrates.

Next, the new sherries are fortified with brandy, the finos being brought up to about 15 per cent alcohol content and the olorosos to 18 per cent. Then the two types are separated and begin a unique aging process in which they are blended with progressively older sherries in an arrangement of casks called a 'solera'. Eventually the new wines mellow and acquire the uniform character which the producer seeks to reproduce from year to year. They are then drawn off for shipment to world markets after being fortified with additional brandy to a maximum of about 20 per cent alcohol.

Grapes spread on round straw mats in the sun, they are sometimes dusted with ◀ *chalky soil*

The sherries of Spain are renowned but, in fact, sherry constitutes less than 5 per cent of Spain's wine output; in production of natural wines (some 600 million gallons per annum), Spain is the third or fourth biggest producer in Europe. Like Italy, Spain has been keeping most of its wines for home consumption, but recently it has begun to export significant quantities of wine besides sherry. The usually good and sometimes exciting quality of these wines, not to mention their modest prices, is earning them an increasingly favorable reputation.

The largest vineyard region is called

Bougainvillia flowering in a Spanish vineyard. The sherry is being 'fortified'

La Mancha, to the southeast of Madrid. The land is a hot, arid plateau, suited to sturdy rather than sophisticated vines. Because of the ample sunshine, the grapes (predominantly red) ripen thoroughly; but their high sugar content makes them deficient in acid, yielding a wine which is rich enough in alcohol but lacks bouquet and tastes a little flat. This is Spain's largest source of 'vin ordinaire', accounting for about one-third of the national output. The chief wine town of La Mancha is Valdepeñas and many of the wines from this region bear that name.

Along the east coast, near Barcelona, is Spain's second largest wine region: Catalonia. Its three districts of Priorato, Tarragona and Panadés produce nearly 20 per cent of the country's table wines. Both reds and whites are made, but the latter are the most in demand. A few of the white wines are sweet.

Among the smaller wine regions is Rioja but it is certainly the most important. Located near the French border, it is the source of the finest dry reds from Spain. It enjoys the best climate, has reasonably good soil and its vintners traditionally have set high standards. The

The arid land in this Spanish vineyard grows hardy wines which are very sophisticated. The continual sun makes the grapes thoroughly ripe.

wines are most often compared to those of the Médoc and it is alleged that Bordeaux vintners, driven from their land by the phylloxera epidemic, made important contributions to wine-making in Rioja. Like fine Médoc wines, those of this district often improve in bottle over many years and are well worth investigation because of their superior quality and competitive price.

PART III:

Wines of the United States

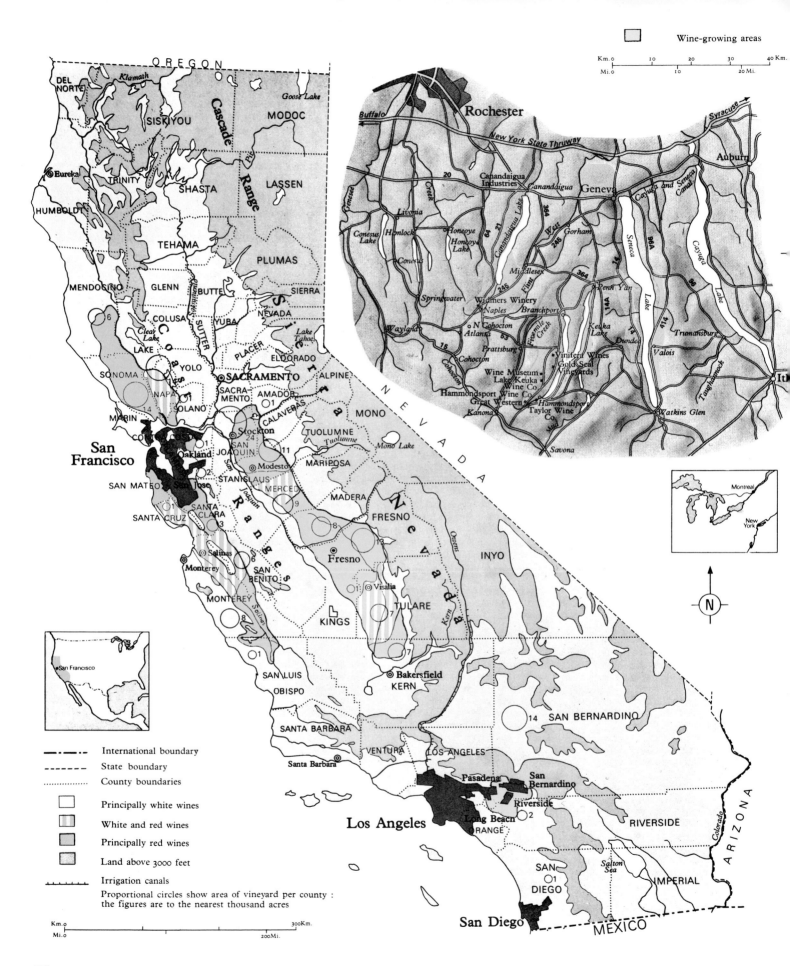

Km.0   10   20   30   40 Km.
Mi.0   10   20 Mi.

OREGON

DEL
NORTE

Klamath

SISKIYOU

Cascade Range

MODOC

Goose Lake

Eureka

TRINITY

SHASTA

LASSEN

HUMBOLDT

TEHAMA

PLUMAS

MENDOCINO

GLENN

BUTTE

SIERRA

Pit

Buffalo   New York State Thruway   Syracuse

Rochester

Auburn

Canandaigua Industries

Canandaigua   Geneva

Cayuga and Seneca Canal

Livonia

Honeoye

Gorham

GLENN

COLUSA

Clear
Lake

LAKE

YUBA

NEVADA

Lake
Tahoe

Conesus
Lake   Hemlock

Honeoye
Lake

West

Seneca

Springwater

Widmers Winery

Flint

Penn Yan

Naples   Branchport

Finger

Keuka Lake

Cayuga Lake

SONOMA

NAPA

YOLO

PLACER

ELDORADO

Wayland

N Cohocton
Atlanta

Dundee

Trumansburg

Valois

MARIN

SOLANO

SACRAMENTO

AMADOR

ALPINE

Prattsburg

Cohocton

Vinifera Wines
Gold Seal
Vineyards

14

SACRA-
MENTO

CALAVERAS

MONO

15

Cohocton

Wine Museum
Lake Keuka
Wine Co.

San
Francisco

COSTA

Oakland

Stockton

TUOLUMNE

Tuolumne

Hammondsport Wine Co.
Great Western

Hammondsport
Taylor Wine
Co.

Watkins Glen

Ith

24

SAN
JOAQUIN

11

Mono Lake

Kanona

Savona

SAN MATEO

San Jose

STANISLAUS

Modesto

MARIPOSA

2

SANTA
CRUZ

SANTA
CLARA

3

MERCED

9

MADERA

Montreal

Salinas

Monterey

SAN
BENITO

8

FRESNO

13

New
York

MONTEREY

8

Salinas

Fresno

INYO

Owens

1   Visalia

TULARE

7

KINGS

N

SAN LUIS

OBISPO

7

Kern

7

Bakersfield

KERN

SANTA BARBARA

14   SAN BERNARDINO

VENTURA

LOS ANGELES

Santa Barbara

Pasadena   San
Bernardino

International boundary

State boundary

County boundaries

Principally white wines

White and red wines

Principally red wines

Land above 3000 feet

Irrigation canals

Proportional circles show area of vineyard per county:
the figures are to the nearest thousand acres

Los Angeles

Long Beach

ORANGE

Riverside

2

RIVERSIDE

Colorado

ARIZONA

SAN
DIEGO

1

Salton
Sea

IMPERIAL

San Francisco

Km.0   300 Km.
Mi.0   200 Mi.

San Diego

MEXICO

Nearly 100 years ago, one of the leading figures in California's fledgling wine industry gave this stern assessment of his fellow countrymen:

'The average American is a whisky-drinking, water-drinking, coffee-drinking, tea-drinking and consequently dyspepsia-inviting subject who does not know the use or value of pure, light wine, taken at the proper time and in moderate quantities.'

Today, there is increasing evidence that this harsh judgement is outmoded. Of course, there have always been partisans of the grape in the U.S. consisting mostly of European-born Americans, a coterie of well-to-do and sometimes well informed gourmets, and alcoholics too poor to afford hard liquor. But the general public, preoccupied with coffee and cola, beer and booze has demonstrated its contempt for these minorities by using epithets like 'iago', 'snob' and 'wino'. Sometime in the 1960's, these words began to recede from the national lexicon. America was starting to share the European appreciation for wine.

The causes of this conversion are not entirely clear. Certainly, a growth in affluence and leisure time have played a part. Increased travel to western Europe and a new found interest in its culinary traditions have also been important. Other factors have been a recognition of the healthful properties of wine compared to spirits, and the emergence of a generation of Americans whose attitudes toward alcohol are no longer seriously influenced by the Prohibition experiment.

Whatever the causes, the effects of the new fondness for wine are already apparent. Twenty years ago, wine consumption in this country was about one gallon per adult per year. Today, that figure has more than doubled. To be sure, U.S. wine consumption per head of population is still only about one-twentieth that of France or Italy. But the rate of increase in the last few years has been so substantial that the prospect of equalling Europe's per capita consumption of wine early in the next century no longer seems outlandish.

The dramatic increase in wine consumption among the country's young adults certainly points in this direction. For some, this shift may be only a gesture of protest against the stronger beverages

Recently, there has been a rapid growth in U.S. vineyard acreage. In this California vineyard new grapes are seen against a background of mature vines

used by their parents. But the majority appear to be enjoying wines for reasons no more reactionary or complex than those espoused by generations of Europeans.

Another sign of the public's new enchantment with wine is the popularity of winetasting parties. Wine study groups now exist in virtually every corner of the nation. Department stores report a substantial sale of wine publications and an insatiable demand for wine glasses. Around the San Francisco Bay area, the bumper-to-bumper weekend traffic to the principal vineyards proves that the wineries are coming to rival

the park system as a tourist attraction.

This rapidly expanding popular interest in wine is matched by a growth in the U.S. wine industry that is so vigorous it might be described as an explosion. New vineyards are being planted at a record rate and long established properties are being replanted with improved grape varieties. At the wineries, the changes are even more startling. Important improvements in the ancient process of converting grapes to wine are being made and a wide variety of new equipment and techniques are being introduced.

This transformation of the American

Native American grapes in a Vineyard high above Lake Keuka in New York State

wine industry requires money — lots of it — but there seems to be no shortage. The last few years have witnessed significant changes in the economic organization of the industry as many family-owned wineries have been taken over by giant corporations with the capital required for growth and modernization.

So far, this marriage between the financiers and the vintners seems to be working out quite well. A few established wine properties apparently have been exploited by new owners seeking to turn a fast dollar. But most corporations have understood that quality winemaking requires patience. They realize that in the long run, their own commercial success will depend upon how well their wines are made.

Consequently, most vintners have found themselves in the enviable position of being left alone to pursue their traditional art, but with the benefit of more grapes and better equipment. The result is a winemaking revolution whose most striking aspect is that both quantity and quality are improving simultaneously and neither is advancing at the expense of the other.

THE HISTORY OF AMERICAN WINES

Twenty years ago, or even ten, virtually nobody would have believed that the U.S. would by now hold a significant place among the nations that produce and consume wine. This progress is all the more remarkable in view of the history of American winemaking — a story in two parts, reflecting the separate experiences of vintners in the eastern and western U.S. This fundamental division is the result of different grape-growing environments on either side of the continent. In a sense, the country has two wine industries, one uniquely American, the other more closely related to the European tradition.

The Eastern Experience

When European settlers first arrived on America's eastern seaboard, they were amazed at the profusion of wild grapes. They were sure that they had indeed found the 'promised land' and set about making wine almost immediately. A letter of 1606, attributed to Captain John Smith, describes the making of 20 gallons, presumably from native Virginia grapes. The Jamestown Colonial Assembly is known to have offered a prize for winemaking in 1658.

But the wines that were derived from these wild vines were distasteful to European palates. Thinking that European grape varieties would surely prosper in a landscape so overlaid with vines, the settlers tried importing plants from their native countries to establish an American wine industry on European foundations. These plants were all members of the classic, wine-grape family *vitis vinifera.* Without exception, the efforts to transplant European grapes to American soil failed. Despite the support of Lord De La Warr and Charles II of England, and diligent experiments by such notables as William Penn and Thomas Jefferson, the European grapes simply would not grow in the climate of eastern America.

It was not until the beginning of the 19th century that Americans developed grape varieties suited both to their palates and to the stern growing conditions of the eastern states. These vines were the result of cross-breeding between various native American strains from the grape families *vitis labrusca, vitis rotoundifolia, vitis rioaria,* and *vitis aestivalis.* These new grapes were given names like Alexander, Catawba, Isabella and Scuppernong and, by mid-century, vintners were raising new varieties such as Concord, Delaware and Diamond.

Some authorities have argued that in fact the grape varieties changed less than American tastes, because as their politics and palates became less European, Americans became more tolerant of wines that could be made from native varieties. In any event, the wine industry envisioned by the colonists finally got under way in the early 1800s on American — not European — grape stock. As a result, its products were unique among the wines of the world and largely remain so today.

The most extensive vineyards of the new industry were laid out in New York and Ohio, but Pennsylvania, New Jersey, Virginia and the Carolinas also had significant plantings. During the 19th century, commercial viniculture spread to Mis-

California vineyard workers loading freshly-picked grapes to take to the winery. This work is more often done by mechanical harvesters

souri, Kansas, Illinois, Indiana and Michigan. But their entire output was soon to be dwarfed by a single state on the other side of the continent — California.

Wine in the West

The Spanish colonists of Mexico were committed to the idea of a major wine industry in the New World long before the first English settlers arrived in Virginia. The vanguard of this enterprise was the Catholic church and vineyards were established at each of its new missions. The first Franciscan mission to be founded in what later became the U.S.

The Berringer Brothers winery in California's Napa Valley, one of a series of famous vineyard estates founded in the San Francisco Bay area late in the 19th century

was at San Diego in 1769. Over the next 60 years, 20 more missions were established in a chain that extended north to the San Francisco Bay area.

From the beginning the missionaries encountered none of the difficulties experienced by the eastern colonists. The grape that the Catholic friars cultivated — still known and grown as the 'mission grape' — was a derivative of those first brought from Spain and it did well in the benign California climate. It did not produce a very sophisticated wine, but the grapes were hardy, prolific and European in character.

By the 1820's, Spanish and ecclesiastical power were on the wane in the American west, but the potential of the wine industry had been amply demonstrated. Small commercial vineyards were established in the San Diego and Los Angeles areas and new settlers with winemaking experience in Europe added impetus to the movement.

Most important among these was an enterprising young Frenchman with the appropriate name of Jean-Louis Vignes. In addition to founding the first sizable and highly prosperous vineyards in California, Vignes brought new vines from his native Bordeaux and introduced the practice of aging wine in oak barrels.

His success attracted other settlers to winemaking and with surprising speed viniculture expanded north from the Los Angeles basin to San Francisco Bay. The Bay area offered superior growing conditions and a ready wine market as a result of the Gold Rush boom of 1849. Among those who flocked to San Francisco during this period was an extraordinarily talented and energetic Hungarian nobleman named Agoston Haraszthy.

Known today as the Father of California viniculture, Haraszthy established his Buena Vista vineyard at Sonoma, north of San Francisco Bay, in 1857. Within two years, he had planted over 110,000 vines, written a definitive treatise on winemaking and won a statewide competition. By 1861, he had demonstrated the feasibility of hillside planting, prompted the founding of an agricultural college and proved that redwood could be substituted for the more expensive oak in wine vats and casks.

In only four years, Haraszthy had become the dominant figure in western winemaking and was commissioned by the California legislature to go to Europe to study vinicultural techniques and to bring back additional vine stock. In 1862, he returned with a staggering collection of 100,000 cuttings from 300 grape varieties.

Seven years later, Haraszthy died with many of his hopes still unfulfilled, but his prodigious contributions had transformed winegrowing in California into an important new industry. By massively importing high quality European wines, he had set California on a different path from that of the eastern states and also prepared it for competition with other countries employing these classic grape varieties.

Prohibition

During the remainder of the 19th and early part of the 20th centuries, the new wine industries on both sides of the continent experienced modest growth, tempered by the setbacks that are common to all winegrowing regions. But, in 1919, they were confronted with a disaster far more fundamental than economic depression or blight in the vineyard: wine was made illegal.

At the time there seemed to be no prospect that this radical measure would be temporary. The prohibition was enshrined in the 18th Amendment to the Constitution and backed by a strictly worded enforcement law known as the Volstead Act. As it turned out, this 'noble experiment' lasted only 14 years. But that period was sufficient to do enormous damage to American viniculture.

Many wine producers went out of business almost immediately. In 1919 in New York, for example, there were more than 50 wineries in the Finger Lakes region; today there are less than a dozen. In California, the reduction was equally dramatic and only about 100 wineries survived the dry years. Vineyards were replanted with table grapes and other fruits. Winery equipment fell into decay, vinicultural research stopped and vintners turned to other work or went back to Europe.

Of more lasting importance, however, was the way Prohibition crippled the

Classic European grapes growing in a California vineyard. Their success set California on an entirely different path than the eastern states which were committed to native grape varieties

American taste for wine. Before 1919, steady growth in wine consumption in the U.S. suggested that wine would continue to grow in popularity as it had in other wine-producing nations. But the Volstead Act not only arrested this growth, it turned the public toward distilled spirits.

For law-breakers, wine was undesirable because of its bulk and low alcohol content. Pocket flasks of high-proof liquor became the rage and by the time of Repeal in 1933, the cocktail party had become a national institution. Ironically, Prohibition's legacy was to discredit the name of wine and to make America among the world leaders in hard liquor consumption.

Renaissance

The recovery from the experiment in abstinence was slow. Wineries could be rebuilt and vineyards planted in relatively

short order. New people could be trained and research resumed. But the major task was re-educating the public. Prohibition was followed by the Great Depression and the reputation of American wine was dealt another blow when most vintners turned to making brandy-laced, sweet wines from low quality, bulk production grapes. These inferior wines, marketed as sherry, port and sauterne, but known collectively as 'sneaky pete', had a ready market because they were the cheapest alcohol a down-and-out public could afford.

With the recovery from the Depression, the fashion for cocktails revived. For most people, wine had become a dim memory and lacked the glamor of the more potent drinks. This preference accelerated during World War II and by 1945, it appeared that Americans had forever lost the habit of drinking wine.

The renaissance that is so visible today

The famed Inglenook winery north of San Francisco — one of those that survived the unfortunate experiment with Prohibition

probably began about 1960, but the shift in taste toward wine was not immediately apparent. In fact, it was not until 1967 that the public's consumption of the natural, dry table wines that are the norm in most wine-drinking nations exceeded that of 'sneaky pete'.

Since this shift occurred, the sale of these natural wines has been increasing by about 10 per cent each year. A major transformation in the American attitude toward wine is clearly under way, and it is causing fundamental changes in the American wine industry as U.S. vintners strive to meet the public's new demand for more and higher quality wines.

The Revolution in American Winemaking

Until very recently, U.S. winemakers were governed by the need to interest an essentially non-wine-drinking society and to convince Americans to make wine the routine accompaniment to meals that it is in other western countries. To achieve these goals, they have followed two maxims: keep it simple and inexpensive. The result has been wines that generally are not comparable to the best European vintages and certainly not representative of the potential of American winemaking.

For many years, a good deal of American wine was vinified from such inferior grapes as the Thompson Seedless. Such varieties were a legacy from Prohibition when many vineyards were replanted with table grapes. Their use kept down the cost of wine and was acceptable as long as the public demanded nothing better. Many American vineyards have richer soil and warmer average temperatures than the best wine-growing districts in Europe. As a result, most grapes harvested in this country have tended to be higher in sugar and lower in that natural acidity that accounts for the dry, crisp character of many of the finer European vintages. American vintners have long understood the techniques for increasing acidity, but for a public that was just learning to drink wine, they tended to leave their products on the sweet side.

For similar reasons, most U.S. winemakers did relatively little to develop richer character and greater keeping qualities in American wines, though they knew these could be increased by the prolonged fermentation and aging techniques practiced in Europe.

The wine industry believed that most Americans wanted their wines on the light side and for immediate consumption, and would not pay the extra price that such quality winemaking practices require.

The past few years have witnessed a sudden change in these attitudes. The day is now well passed when the principal goal of American vintners was to convince their reluctant and uninterested countrymen to drink wine. In fact, the industry can hardly produce enough to meet the new demand. Moreover, this demand is particularly strong for wines made from premium grape varieties that are dry on the palate, rich in flavor and bouquet and have the complexity that comes with age.

In effect, the American public has challenged the industry to come forward with a range of wines comparable in quality to the best from Europe. To meet this challenge, a revolution in the American approach to winemaking is required. There are at least three good reasons to believe that it will be accomplished.

First, the public interest in wine appears to be strong and unflagging. Admittedly, the evidence that Americans as a whole have finally become enamoured of wine is recent. But the sustained growth in wine consumption over the past decade does not have the earmarks of a fad. It appears, rather, to represent a fundamental and permanent shift in popular taste, corroborated by the recent phenomenal growth of interest in more sophisticated foods. Nor is there any lack of money to back this new-found enthusiasm for wine. Major financial institutions are bullish about the future and corporations like Hueblein, National Distillers, Nestlé, Pepsi-Cola and Seagrams all have competed vigorously to get their piece of the action.

A second reason for confidence in the future is the absence of significant legal obstacles to new directions in winemaking. Unlike more established vinicultural nations, the U.S. is not trying to preserve high standards of quality, it is trying to achieve them. Of course, the pure food and drug laws govern wine production and there are still some curious legacies of the Prohibition era that restrict the sale of wine. But there is no code like the Appellation Controllée system of France that limits the sorts of grapes that may be planted or the techniques of vinification that may be employed. The young American wine industry essentially remains free to realize its potential.

Finally, there is probably no wine-producing country whose vintners are more open to innovation in winemaking. While traditional vinicultural practice is still deeply respected, there is also, in every American vineyard, keen interest in experimentation and in new methods. Quantity and quality in winemaking are not seen as incompatible.

This revolution in American viniculture is not some hoped-for development of the far distant future. Already, new wines have been marketed that attest to this revolution in American viniculture. In research laboratories, in the vineyards and in the wineries, extraordinary developments are taking place.

The Revolution in Research
During the years when the future of American wine was in doubt, the basis for the transformation of the industry was being laid through research. The principal institutions involved were the University of California at Davis, Cornell University and the Geneva Experimental Station in New York State. Associated with these institutions, or working independently at their own vineyards, have

This vineyard in California's Great Central Valley has richer soil and higher temperature than Europe's best wine-producing regions. But these 'better' conditions result in less distinguished wine

Splendid California vineyards like this one are the result of thorough research into climate and soil conditions and the choice of the most appropriate grape varieties

This California vineyard worker is pruning wood from the vine so that more of the plant's energy will be devoted to high quality grapes. This task is universal and unlikely to be mechanized since human judgement is required for best results

survive over the long term. Skilled viniculturalists have succeeded in producing superior white wines from European grapes in small quantities, but there is little prospect of large-scale production. The development of the so-called French-American varieties, however, seem much more promising. These new hybrid grapes result from continued cross-breeding of European and American vines (on both sides of the Atlantic) and in the last 10 years, varieties that retain the hardness, but eliminate the 'wild' aroma and flavor of the native eastern grapes have been widely planted in commercial vineyards. These hybrids can be grown easily in large quantities and, most important, they produce a wine with European grape character. Thus, by a strange twist of history, the French-American varieties that were developed in Europe to simplify the laborious grafting process necessitated by an American root louse may prove to be the salvation of the eastern wine industry. They can lay the foundation for a whole new family of varietal wines as well as reduce the grapey quality of traditional eastern wines through blending. Their hardiness suggests that they could be cultivated over a far wider area. New vineyards in Maryland, West Virginia, Kentucky and other states have already pointed the way.

The Revolution in the Vineyard

Most American vineyards look like those the world over and are cultivated in essentially the same annual cycle of pruning, ploughing, frost protection, spraying and harvesting. But U.S. vintners are making innovations in these basic activities that, if not unique to this country, are probably more rapidly and widely adopted here than elsewhere.

Beginning with the soil, American growers are employing deep fumigation techniques to guard against the fatal phylloxera louse and other root diseases. Knowing that some of the world's finest wines spring from the poorest soil, some growers are experimenting with leaner land or with making their present vineyards less fecund. Others are moving to higher ground where their vines may benefit from a colder climate.

On the mechanical side, new equipment is being used to establish vineyards in a fraction of the time required

been such figures as Bioletti, Cruess, Winkler, Olmo and Amerine in the West and Wellington, Fournier, Greyton Taylor, Frank and Wagner in the East.

In California, much time has been spent discovering which of the classic European grape stock is best suited to particular areas of the state. Variants have been developed with improved quality, higher yield and greater resistance to heat and certain diseases. A great deal of effort has also gone into developing new types of machinery for vineyard and winery operations.

For vinicultural purposes, California research scientists have divided the state into five zones, representing the full range of climates in which wine grapes will flourish. Much of the state's most prestigious vineyards are in Zones 1 and 2, the coolest areas. The same research

also has shown that there are extensive areas with this superior climate in California that are not yet planted with wine grapes. These can provide the industry with the room for expansion it now needs.

In the East, research has focused on developing grapes that will make wine closer to the world standard. Eastern vintners have made significant advances in vineyard and winery techniques over the years, but their products are still made largely from domesticated native grapes. As a result, eastern wines are increasingly regarded as curiosities in a market in which 85 per cent of the wines sold (70 per cent from California and 15 per cent from abroad) are made from *vitis vinifera* grapes.

Most eastern vintners recognize that they must improve their grape stock to

Many California vineyards, such as this one in the newly developed Monterrey district, have irrigation systems arranged on stakes above the vines to provide artificial rainfall, pesticides and frost-protection with unprecedented efficiency

by hand labor. Overhead irrigation systems (some of them computer-controlled) are now being used to simulate rainfall in the amounts and at the times required. These systems are a major improvement over the older techniques using pipes or ditches, since they can also be used to apply chemical sprays and to moderate adverse weather. When vineyard temperatures become too high, an artificial 'shower' can be created to reduce the heat. When frost threatens, the system can cover the grapes with a thin jacket of ice that, far from harming the fruit, protects it from the colder outside atmosphere. This technique elimi-

nates the need for smoke pots, wind machines and other traditional frost protection equipment.

Another innovation of American vintners is the mechanical harvester. It was developed in the late '50s, primarily because fewer U.S. citizens were willing to pick grapes. Designing an effective substitute for manual labor was complicated because of the vulnerability of grapes and vines to mechanical handling, the variations in vineyard layouts and the need to deliver only cleanly picked fruit to the winery. Early efforts concentrated on developing grapes with long, fragile stems and machines that

could slice, suck or beat the fruit from the vine.

Recently, machines have been developed that require no genetic change in the grape and can pick more undamaged fruit at greater speed than is humanly possible. These harvesters straddle a row of vines and, as the machine moves forward, a series of flexible rods (about 1 foot long and 1 inch in diameter) oscillates through the plants from each side, nudging the bunches of ripe fruit so that they fall onto a conveyor belt. These mechanical 'fingers' do not harm the vine because their reverse movement is counteracted by the forward speed of the entire apparatus, keeping their impact on the plants to a minimum. Fortunately, this invention has come at a time when vineyards are being replanted with higher quality grapes and new properties are being established, permitting a layout of new rows and trellises appropriate for mechanical harvesting.

Although these machines are a major boon to growers, they ultimately will rebound to the advantage of the consumer, who should enjoy better wines because of time saved between picking and fermentation of the grape. In traditional harvesting, the newly picked fruit sits in lugs until it can be transported to the winery, and there it may wait again until it can be piled in a fermenter. Each moment of delay means a loss in the freshness of the grapes and a corresponding reduction in the quality of the wine.

Moreover, in the traditional harvest, many grapes break as they are picked and moved about. With exposure to oxygen, they discolor and lose fragrance as quickly as an apple does once it has been bitten; the warmer the weather, the quicker harmful bacteria multiply. Bacterial growth can be arrested at the winery with a generous dose of chemicals, but this prophylactic measure can have its own ill effect upon the wine.

Mechanical harvesting reduces these problems significantly. A single machine not only picks vines much faster (it can cover about an acre per hour), but simultaneously blows away any stray leaves, dust and insects before conveying the fruit to large containers moving parallel with the harvester. As soon as the containers are full, they are fork-lifted onto trucks and taken directly to the winery. Because the harvesters work at a predictable rate and can pick both night and day, winery operations can be scheduled more precisely and the risk that no fermenting tanks will be free is curtailed.

Several American winemakers are experimenting with even quicker procedures. One is called 'vineyard crushing', a technique that in effect brings part of the winery to the vineyard. Destemming and crushing equipment, usually found only at the winery, is modified and attached to the mechanical harvester so that, as the grapes are picked, they are stemmed, crushed and transferred to tanks mounted on the har-

A mechanical harvester by stainless steel storage tanks, two key elements in the revolution in American wine-making

vester. These tanks are filled with carbon dioxide gas to create a sterile, oxygen-free environment and when they are full, the crushed grapes are pumped into tank trucks, still under a protective cover of carbon dioxide, and taken to the fermenter. As a result, these vineyard-crushed grapes arrive at the winery far fresher and cleaner than any that winemakers have worked with in the past.

The first commercial application of this technique was made by Mirassou Vineyards of California in the fall of 1970. Vineyard-crushed wines are now available from several of the leading California vintners. While this revolutionary technique must await more widespread

use before its ultimate importance can be assessed, there are many vintners who already share Mirassou's belief that this innovation could prove to be the most significant advance in winemaking since the introduction of the cork 200 years ago.

The Revolution in the Winery

In wineries around the world, the great enemies have always been oxygen, high temperatures and a host of bacteria that like to feed on wine. Today, the principal weapons used in combating these are inert gases, refrigeration machinery and stainless steel. Nowhere are they applied on a larger scale than in the U.S.

109

A tank truck delivers 'vineyard-crushed' grapes to the fermentation facility at California's Mirassou Vineyards. This new system significantly reduces grape spoilage and results in greatly improved wines

Oxygen is vital to certain phases of winemaking, particularly in maturing red wines. But, for the most part, the vintner must strive to keep oxygen at bay because, like most fruit products, wine will spoil with exposure to the atmosphere. Until recently the vintner's defense against this threat was essentially passive; he would try to make winery equipment as airtight as possible by using water seals, and by regularly filling with more wine the air spaces that developed through evaporation. Today, vintners are taking a more active approach. By using certain gases (principally nitrogen and carbon dioxide) that have no effect on the aroma or taste of wine, they can displace oxygen and any infectious organisms in the atmosphere.

In modern American wineries, these gases are being used more and more. When grapes first arrive at the stemmer—crusher, they are often covered with a protective blanket of inert gas. If there is a delay before fermentation, the grape juice can be kept in suspended animation by displacing the air in a holding tank with carbon dioxide. While wine is actively fermenting it produces its own carbon-dioxide protection, but as this process subsides, the vintner can add more inert gas. The same technique can be used while the wine is being clarified, aged and stored, and also for purifying wine bottles before they are filled. All of this helps to make wine of higher quality, that ages better.

Refrigeration is another versatile and increasingly-applied technique. In the classic wine districts of Europe, refrigeration is not as important since the weather is generally cool in fall and winter when winery operations are at their peak. But as viniculture has spread to hotter climates, techniques for dissipating warmth have become increasingly important. This is particularly true in California where inland winter temperatures are not far from those of summer in the Mosel or Champagne districts of France.

The need for refrigeration during fermentation can be critical. When grape sugar is converted into equal parts of alcohol and carbon dioxide, one of the chief by-products is heat. If this heat cannot be dissipated into the surrounding atmosphere, the temperature of the fer-

Winery workers have regularly to check the condition of maturing wines and replace any losses through evaporation

menting grape juice will rise and kill the yeast that sustains the conversion. When this occurs, the wine is said to be 'stuck' and, although fermentation may be restarted after a drop in temperature and the addition of fresh yeast, the quality of the wine is never the same.

To keep temperatures as low and as even as possible, winery buildings have traditionally been constructed with thick stone walls or built into hillsides. When more cooling was needed, the usual agent has been water, sprayed or circulated in pipes around the wine tanks, or

pumped through coils of pipe lowered into the wine.

But, no matter what method was used, its effectiveness depended on the temperature of the water from the local stream, pond or public water system.

Refrigeration has changed all that. Water or other cooling agents can be chilled to the appropriate temperatures and fermentation tanks can be constructed with walls incorporating the refrigerant material. Even the room in which the fermentation tanks are located can be air-conditioned.

For countries whose vineyards have hot fall climates, artificial cooling equipment is essential to successful fermentation. But wineries around the world — even those in the coolest European districts — are also installing refrigeration plants. This not only frees the vintner from dependence upon favorable weather conditions, but it also permits him to use temperature control creatively. Instead of being at the mercy of the climate, the vintner can choose processing temperatures based upon the variety and condition of the grapes with which he is

New wine being pumped from the fermentation vats to stainless steel storage tanks at a modern California winery

working, and the style and quality of wine that he hopes to produce.

The creative role of refrigeration can already be seen at several progressive wineries in California. Vintners there have discovered that one way of improving the acidity of their white wines is to reduce the loss of volatile acids that inevitably occurs in the heat of conventional fermentation. This can be done by fermenting white wine grape juice at temperatures between 40°–50°. The process is more expensive than normal fermentation because special strains of yeast must be employed to sustain the conversion of sugar at these low temperatures and because the change from grape juice to wine may take several months. However, the improvement in the finished product is so remarkable that this technique is likely to find increasing favor among those attempting to make the finest California white wines.

Artificial cooling equipment is also being employed at other points in winemaking. At some wineries, grapes are chilled on arrival. This reduces spoilage if there is a delay before fermentation, and yields a wine with more natural grape character. Similarly, if grape juice is chilled before fermentation, solid particles are precipitated and the resulting wine is cleaner. Refrigeration can also be used to clarify wine after fermentation, thereby reducing the need for chemical additives or filtering.

It has long been recognized that different wines require different time periods and temperatures to mature properly. Giving wines the time needed for proper aging has seldom been a problem, but temperature is another story. Those vintners fortunate enough to have deep cellars or hillside caves can age their whites there, and keep their reds slightly warmer within the winery building. But most winemakers are limited to a common aging room in which the temperature is seldom appropriate for all of their wines.

Refrigeration equipment permits a vintner to age his wines in a particular room kept at the right temperature. In addition, when the aging is completed, the wines may be transferred to refrigerated tanks to be kept in good condition until bottling.

Another major change in the American

Refrigerated storage tanks permit vintners to keep their wine outside at ideal temperatures and avoid the cost of large buildings for aging their wines

wine industry is that steel is now superseding wood in many wineries. Wood has long been considered essential to quality winemaking, but recent research has shown that there is no appreciable advantage in using wood in any phase of winemaking except aging. Moreover, wood is hard to keep clean. Whenever a wooden wine vessel is emptied, it must be laboriously scoured and fumigated with sulphur wicks. Although there are chemicals with which to doctor a wine infected during processing, none can be used without detriment to the final product.

Thus, progressive wineries around the world, including such exalted properties as Château Latour in Bordeaux, are turning to other materials. Glass, concrete and various forms of rubber, plastic and polyurethane have been tried, but the preferred material is stainless steel. It has no adverse effect upon wine, it is extremely durable and, above all, it is easy to keep clean. In the most advanced American wineries, stainless steel is used in grape receiving troughs, in stem-crushers, presses, fermenters, holding tanks and the piping that connects so many components of a winemaking system.

In such modern plants, wooden equipment is confined to containers used for maturing new wine and here, too, there is change. Many American vintners are shifting from redwood to oak casks, particularly for aging white wines. The oak comes from a wide variety of sources, including France, Italy, Yugoslavia and the southeastern U.S., and vintners are hoping to find which kind is compatible with their different wines. A considerable investment is involved in this conversion — further evidence of the quest for quality in the American wine industry.

Three other types of equipment deserve mention. The first is the wine press. Several new systems are now employed to separate the grape juice from solid matter when making white wine. The new wine presses aim to apply pressure that is specifically suited to particular grapes and avoid crushing seeds and other solids which might impart unwanted flavors, scents or colors to the wine. This more gentle pressing process produces white wines that are more sophisticated and truer to their grape parentage.

Another important new device in the

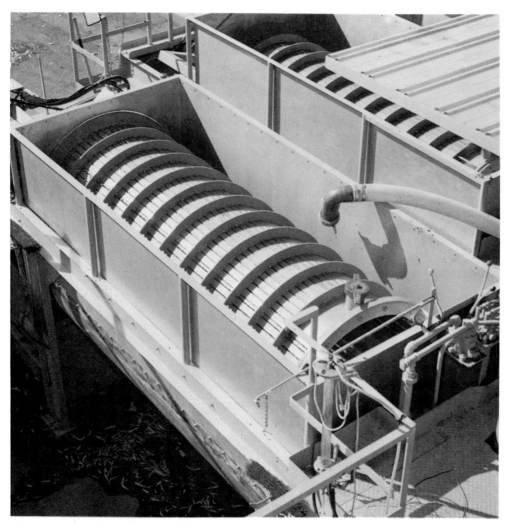

Here the grapes are received from the vineyards and stemmed and crushed

production of improved white wines is the centrifuge that separates those small, solid particles that remain in grape juice after pressing. Pioneered by German vintners, centrifuging (before and after fermentation) produces wines of markedly improved clarity and taste, with no loss in the natural characteristics of the grape.

Finally, some American red wines are now being improved by the use of a rotating fermentation tank. During fermentation red wines gain their color and several other characteristics from contact between the essentially colorless grape juice and the highly pigmented grape skins. However, this contact is limited by the tendency of the skins to rise to the top of the tank with the heat of fermentation, forming a nearly solid cap. Traditionally, this cap is broken by punching the solid matter down into the juice at regular intervals, or by pumping the juice from the bottom of the tank and hosing it over the cap. The work is hard and the wine can be spoiled through over-exposure to oxygen.

A fermentation tank that can be rotated periodically about a horizontal axis is an effective solution to these problems because it mixes juice and skins thoroughly to give red wines of deep color, rich character and long life. It speeds fermentation so the vintner need not compromise the quality of one red wine by hurrying to make room for another.

Romanticists may complain that these new machines, stainless steel tanks and elaborate refrigeration equipment are making American wineries look more and more like petro-chemical processing plants. But the proof is in the bottle and these new techniques are undoubtedly an important factor promoting a rapid improvement in the quality of American wines.

The Language of American Wine Labels

The labelling of grape wines produced in the U.S. is unique in many respects. It is a system whose essential simplicity was born from the need to be easily understood by a nation with a limited familiarity with wine. Although the system is still evolving to meet the rapid changes that are occuring in wine technology and in consumer tastes, it is widely applied throughout the country's scattered vineyard regions. Much of the terminology has been adapted from that in use in Europe. Basically, American vintners classify their wines according to the four recognized categories of grape wines: natural, sparkling, fortified and flavored.

Natural Wine

Most winemaking nations employ a place-name system in identifying their natural wines. That is, each wine is named for the particular vineyard, township, district or region in which it was produced. Inevitably, this has resulted in thousands of different names for wines that are essentially similar.

Such a system worked well when vineyards served nearby communities and their inhabitants knew from personal experience that certain localities had the growing conditions to make good wines. But, today, with the distribution of wines outside their areas of production and even beyond national borders, the direct association between the name of a place and the character of its wines is lost on most people. Only by tedious hit-or-miss experience and by lengthy study, can today's consumer make an intelligent choice from among the hundreds of

A winery worker pumps fermenting red wine from the bottom of the vat over the mass of grape skins which has risen to the top. This improved the flow of color and other important ingredients from the skins to the grape juice

a varietal wine is usually much higher than this minimum. These wines are more expensive than generics, but in addition to being made from premium grapes, they usually receive considerably more care in production. Varietals are the wines on which most American vintners stake their reputation.

This generic/varietal system of naming natural wines is admirably simple, and allows vintners to indicate the individual characteristics of their wines, even if the dominant name on the label is also used by many other producers. The one unfortunate exception to this uncluttered approach is that some proprietors have devised proprietary names for their wines that they hope will have commercial appeal e.g., 'Château La France', 'Rococo' or 'Merry-Go-Round'. None of the wines marketed so far under such labels has been of consequence and it is to be hoped that the practice will be discontinued.

In addition to their generic/varietal description, American labels specify the wine's alcoholic content and its place of origin. Certain vinicultural districts in each state have gained recognition over the years as being superior. If at least 75 per cent of the grapes from which a wine is derived come from one of these districts, the producer may cite the district name, such as 'Finger Lakes' or 'Napa Valley'. Wines that do not meet this criterion are simply labeled with the state name. If less than 75 per cent of a wine is derived from grapes grown in any one state, it can only be designed as 'American'.

The degree to which the producer of a wine has exercised direct control over all phases of its production is also indicated on the label. If a wine is made entirely from grapes grown on the producer's property, and all stages of its vinification and cellaring are carried out under his supervision, the label may carry the words *estate bottled*. So far, only a few producers meet this exacting standard. Most good quality wines carry the designation *produced and bottled*, which means that at least 75 per cent of the grapes used in making the wine were grown on the producer's property.

A fundamental difference between European and American winemaking is that in Europe each vintner usually

labels with which he is confronted in a well-stocked wine shop.

The American system for identifying natural wines attempts to reduce this proliferation of place names by giving common names to wines that are of essentially the same character. It also provides the customer with a simple means of distinguishing Americas 'vin ordinaire' from those wines that represent the country's best vinicultural efforts.

General purpose, 'everyday' wines are named after famous types of European wine to which they bear some resemblance, e.g., Burgundy, Chablis or Rhine. These wines are called *generics* and are made from a wide variety of grapes whose high productivity enables the

vintner to keep the cost low. They are widely distributed throughout the country in gallon and half-gallon jugs (as well as the standard one-fifth gallon bottles) and are often good value. The generics have been among the first beneficiaries of the recent improvements in American winemaking.

The best American wines are the *varietals*, named after the varieties of high-quality, low-yield grapes from which they are predominantly made, e.g., Cabernet Sauvignon, Pinot Noir or Chardonnay. To qualify for this designation, at least 51 per cent of a wine must be derived from the grape variety after which it is named. In practice, the percentage of the principal grape in

The best grape varieties bear the least fruit, but make the most sophisticated wines

produces only one wine from those grapes best suited to his individual soil, terrain and climate. For merchandising reasons U.S. vintners usually produce a much broader line of wines. Inevitably, American wineries must buy semi-finished wines from one another to add to those that they have made in insufficient quantity or to fill out their line with wines they cannot make themselves. Such wines are labelled *made and bottled* if at least 10 per cent of the grapes came from the producer's property. If the wine was simply bought from another producer for resale it must be labeled *cellared and bottled* or, simply, *bottled*.

Until recently, most U.S. vintners avoided the European practice of vintage labeling on the grounds that 'every year is a good year'. It is true that growing conditions are more stable, particularly in California, than in many of the world's major wine-growing areas. Nonetheless, American vineyards are no strangers to the droughts, downpours, frosts, hail, fire, insects and labor problems that account for poor grape crops elsewhere.

U.S. vintners have sought to moderate their inevitable variations in their production by blending the output of different years. Their goal, along with others in the American food and beverage industries, has been to market a product known for consistent quality. This policy has good and bad aspects. On the plus side, it puts the producer's business on a more stable basis and offers the customer an exceptionally dependable wine at a steady price; the debit side to this practice is that very little genuinely exciting wine has been reaching the

Principal Western Wines			
Whites		**Reds**	
Varietals	Generics	Varietals	Generics
Chardonnay (or Pinot Chardonnay) Pinot Blanc (or White Pinot)	Chablis or White Burgundy	Pinot Noir Gamay Beaujolais Gamay Noir Gamay Pinot St. George Red Pinot Garignane	Burgundy
Johannisberg (or White Riesling) Emerald Riesling Franken Riesling Grey Riesling Sylvanner Traminer Gewürztraminer	Riesling or Rhine Wine	Cabernet Sauvignon Cabernet (or Cabernet Franc) Ruby Cabernet Merlot Malbec	Claret or Bordeaux
Sweet (Sauvignon Blanc – Sauterne	Sauterne	Aleatico Barbera Charbono Grignolino Nebbiolo	Chianti or Vino Rosso
Sweet Sauvignon Blanc Fumé Blanc (or Dry Sauvignon Blanc) Chenin Blanc (or Pineau de la Loire)	(Loire)	Petit Sirah Grenache Grenoir	(Rhône)
Dry Sémillon	(Graves)	Zinfandel	(Eastern Europe)
French Columbard Folle Blanc	(Charente)	Cabernet Rosé Gamay Rosé Grenache Rosé Grignolino Rosé Petite (Sirah) Rosé Pinot (Noir) Rosé Zinfandel Rosé	Vin Rosé
Muscat de Frontignan (or white Muscat) Moscato di Canelli (or Moscato Amabile) Malvasia Bianca	(Italy)		
Green Hungarian Veltliner	(Eastern Europe)		

American consumer. In order to remove the qualitative lows from a natural production curve, those superior wines which are made in the best years must be sent to the blending tanks, rather than to the market place.

Happily, as the wine industry grows in strength and the wine public in sophistication, an increasing part of America's vineyard output is sold as vintage wine. The criterion for vintage labeling is: to be sold as the product of a single harvest, 100 per cent of the wine must have been made in the year stated on the label. So far, only the better varietal wines are being sold by vintage since their annual variation is more significant than in other, lesser quality wines.

The table lists all the major natural wines (except those with proprietary labels) from America's western vineyards. The varietal wines are listed opposite those generic types to which they most closely relate. For some varietal wines, no generic equivalents are made. Instead, the European wine type to which they generally correspond is listed in parentheses in the generic column.

Among the California white varietal wines, the most important are the Chardonnay and Johannisberg Riesling. They are primarily made from the classic grapes of Burgundy and the Rhine and bear a strong resemblance to the distinguished wines of these regions. In the past, they have tended to have too little acid, but this is being remedied by modifying the fermentation technique.

Other good white varietals are Fumé Blanc, Chenin Blanc, Dry Sémillon, Gewürztraminer, and Moscato di Canelli. Fumé Blanc, similar to the Pouilly-Fumé from the French Loire, is a recent development in California. As in Pouilly, it is made from the sauvignon blanc, a grape usually associated with the wines of Sauternes. Another Loire-type varietal is the Chenin Blanc, a wine that has improved considerably with new methods of vinification. Dry Sémillon has always been a fine, if little recognized, California white – particularly when it comes from the Livermore Valley. The better Gewürztraminers are comparable to their Alsatian counterparts and Moscato can be a delightful dessert wine, like the whites of northern Italy.

California's best red varietal is unquestionably the Cabernet Sauvignon. It differs from the wines of the same grape grown in Bordeaux because the soil and sun of California are more lush than in the Médoc, but with proper vinification and aging, the American version is as impressive as all but the most exalted clarets.

The reputation of the pinot noir grape is not so high. So far this classic grape of Burgundy's Côte d'Or has not done nearly as well in America as the cabernet sauvignon. Some vintners think that the pinot noir could yield outstanding wines if it were raised in cooler climates where the growing season is longer. Others feel that a superior California Burgundy could be made with the Petit Sirah grape, possibly in combination with the pinot noir.

Two other California reds of merit are the Barbera and Zinfandel. Barbera can be a remarkably hearty and fullsome wine, similar to those of the same name from Piedmont in northern Italy. Zinfandel is the archetypical California red. It is so prolific that vintners make it the dominant element in their generics but it has

Principal Eastern Wines			
Varietals			Generics
Native	French American	Vinifera	
Whites			
Delaware Diamond Diana Dutchess	Seyval Blanc	Chardonnay	Chablis
Dutchess Elvira Niagrara Missouri Riesling	Aurora	Johannisberg Riesling	Rhine
Catawba Concord Scuppernong Vergennes			Sauternes
Reds			
Concord Ives	Baco Noir Chelois	Pinot Noir Cabernet Sauvignon	Burgundy Claret
Rosé			
Catawba Isabella	Cascade		Vin Rosé

sufficient vinous character to make it a genuinely interesting varietal.

The table above lists the names of all the major natural wines (except those with proprietary labels) that come from America's eastern vineyards. Eastern varietal wines currently are made from three different grape families, each having distinct characteristics. These are listed in the first three columns opposite those generic wines to which they most closely relate.

The better eastern wines all carry varietal names. Delaware is the most distinguished of the white varietals from native grapes and Diamond is also noteworthy, but it is not widely available since most of it is made into good quality sparkling wines. No satisfying native varietal red is available.

Among French-American varietals, Seyval Blanc and Aurora are the best. Red wines made from the Baco Noir and Chelois (French American) varietals are an improvement on the native reds.

The rare white wines made from *vitis vinifera* grapes are in a different class entirely; the Chardonnays and Johannisburg Rieslings are unquestionably the best American wines made east of California. The reds however, are less successful and those accustomed to California Pinot Noir and Cabernet Sauvignon should not expect too much from their eastern counterparts.

Sparkling Wines

American vintners use three basic techniques for introducing carbon dioxide into natural wines to make them sparkle. They may start a secondary fermentation in bottles of semi-finished, natural wine; they may do the same for wine stored in tanks; or they may simply get carbon dioxide from some outside source and pump it into the wine. These three methods result in sparkling wines that are quite different in quality and cost. Their labeling is also distinctive.

The finest effervescent wines made in America are produced by the first, or bottle-fermented, method that is identical to the technique used in the Champagne region of France (see page 39).

All natural grape wines that go through this classic method of secondary fermentation without being removed from the original bottle are labeled *Naturally Fermented in this Bottle*. The expense of this procedure, that requires over 100 hand operations during a two-year period, is aggravated by a heavy federal tax, making bottle-fermented sparkling wines among the most costly products of American vineyards. Nevertheless, they enjoy a wide and growing favor from a public that appreciates the higher quality that results from this traditional technique.

The buyer who is looking for the real thing, however, must carefully distinguish wines that are labeled *Naturally Fermented in this Bottle* from those that are labeled *Naturally Fermented in the Bottle*. A number of U.S. producers of bottle-fermented sparkling wine are using a new method that reduces the hand labor involved in sediment removal and addition of sugar. Secondary fermentation is still accomplished in the bottle, but when this is complete the newly sparkling wine is transferred under pressure to a tank. Meanwhile the bottles are washed, given the appropriate dose of syrup, then refilled under pressure and corked. Vintners employing this transfer method are permitted to use the phrase *Naturally Fermented in the Bottle*, but this slight semantic difference is important because the wine can suffer as it is exposed to oxygen in the process of moving from bottle to tank and back to bottle.

The second major method of making sparkling wines in America is to induce a secondary fermentation in natural wines stored in tanks rather than bottles. The tanks, that usually contain about 500 gallons of wine, are really nothing more than big bottles and the basic procedures are nor markedly different from those used in bottle fermentation. But there are good reasons why this technique has so far failed to produce wines that are as sophisticated as those produced by the classic method. First, in creating a secondary fermentation in so large a volume of wine, a considerable quantity

Sparkling wine fermentation tanks, such as these seen at the Franzia Brothers winery in California's Great Central Valley, rapidly produce large quantities of bulk process American champagne

of expired yeast and tartrate accumulates at the bottom of the tank. This sediment is proportionately greater than that produced in bottle fermentation and can have adverse effects on flavor and bouquet. Secondly, since it is harder to clear the residual yeasts from tank-fermented sparkling wines, many producers add a bit of sulphur dioxide to guard against a third fermentation that might occur when the sugar syrup is added. Unfortunately, this chemical is particularly obtrusive in the bubbles of an effervescent wine.

After tank fermentation, the wine is transferred to bottles that have already received the required sugar dosage. At this point, as in the transfer of bottle-fermented wine, oxygen exposure is a threat to the wine's quality and some producers again employ sulphur dioxide to guard against oxidation.

All natural wines that have been made sparkling by secondary fermentation in tanks must be labeled *Bulk Process* or *Charmat Process* (named for one of the inventors of this technique). Some producers attempt a little sleight of hand with the public by using phrases like *Naturally Fermented, Bulk Process*.

Tank fermentation is widely used in the production of red and rosé sparkling wines. Because their initial fermentation was 'on the skins', they have a higher alcohol and tannin content than most white wines. This makes them less susceptible to secondary fermentation and harder to clear of sediment. Since both of these problems are more easily handled in large pressurized tanks than in individual bottles, it is rare to find a sparkling red or rosé wine that is bottle-fermented.

The third major method of making wines bubble is to introduce carbon dioxide gas into a natural wine without inducing a secondary fermentation. Essentially, these wines are made in the same way as most carbonated soft drinks. The wine is reduced to near freezing temperature and the gas is pumped in under pressure. After bottling, the wine returns to normal temperature and the gas expands and distributes itself throughout the liquid.

Carbonated wines have two major disadvantages. Their effervescence tends to subside rather quickly, compared with that produced by secondary fermentation and, since it is derived from non-grape sources, the bubbles fail to carry the scent of the grape. All such wines must be labeled *Carbonated*.

Fortified Wines

American fortified wines can be divided into three broad classes: sherry, port and vermouth. For the most part, only a loose relationship exists between these products and the European wines from which they take their names.

For many years, fortified wines were America's 'vin ordinaire'. They were made quickly from low quality, high-yield grapes for a market in which low price and high alcohol content were the principal desiderata. Ever since the mid-1960s, however, Americans have been turning towards the drier natural wines. As a result, the sale of American sherry, port and vermouth has shown a relative decline. Some producers are convinced that the future of these wines depends at least in part, on restoring them to the more specialized role and higher quality of their European counterparts.

A few good fortified wines have already emerged, proving that a qualitative revolution is possible and fortified wines made in bulk are also benefiting from some of the technological advances made in the production of natural wines. In the main, however, these wines have been the least affected by the revolution in American viniculture. They are also behind the times in lacking a standardized labeling that can be understood easily.

The most important class of fortified wines in terms of volume and diversity is sherry. Despite the public's new fondness for natural wines, sherry production in the U.S. is still greater than in Spain itself, and the demand may expand as the enthusiasm for wine grows and apéritif wines become a partial substitute for cocktails. Consistent with the trend towards dryness in natural wines, Americans now prefer drier sherry.

In the U.S., vintners employ the techniques for making fortified wines developed in Spain and Madeira and call the results sherry. The best are made by growing yeast — usually referred to as 'flor' — on the surface of good quality white wines. The yeast culture is started after fermentation is complete and the

wines have received an initial fortification of grape brandy raising their alcohol content to about 15 per cent. The flor may continue to grow for months or even years in partially filled oak barrels of about 50 gallons capacity. When the yeast has done its work, the sherry will have acquired the characteristic Spanish aroma and nutty flavor. It is then cleared and fortified to a strength of up to 20 per cent alcohol.

If the winemaker has gone to this much trouble and expense, he normally continues with the classic sherry procedure and blends the new wine with older vintages in a solera. Such wines generally carry the word *solera* on the label. Unfortunately, however, the use of

this term is no guarantee that the wine is a genuine 'flor', since sherry made by the much more common Madeira or 'baking' method, can also be matured in a solera system. (However, the back label may cast some light on the process used.)

In the baking method, the newly fermented wine (typically a relatively poor white made from Mission or Thompson Seedless grapes) is fortified to an alcohol content of at least 15 per cent to protect it from vinegar bacteria. Then it is placed in large concrete tanks and heated to 120°F–140°F for one to four months. During this process, some wood flavor can be introduced by mixing chips of white oak with the wine. Most of this bulk process sherry receives very little

This sherry cask has a glass end to show the yeast or flor growing on the surface of the new wine

aging after the final clarification and fortification are complete.

Both flor and baked sherry use the same terms to describe degrees of sweetness. The driest are variously labeled as *Dry, Pale Dry* or *Cocktail*. Medium types are often called *Medium*, but also *Fine, Golden* or *Straight*. The sweetest types may be labeled *Sweet*, but more often *Cream* or *Dessert*.

The production of port wines in the U.S. is similar in its fundamentals to the procedures developed in Portugal. However, very few American vintners use the grapes or the aging techniques that have made the fortified wines of Oporto so famous. Red port is usually made from grapes notable for their yield, like the Carignane, that are picked when they have developed a sugar content of about 25 per cent. During fermentation, the winemaker's chief problem is to get enough red pigment from the grape skins before the addition of brandy halts the sugar conversion process.

The clarification and aging for most red ports requires a year or less in concrete tanks. Their color is still bright red at the time of bottling and they are appropriately labeled *ruby port*. Red ports that receive further aging in wood lose some of this bright color and are sold as *tawny port*. Only a handful of American red ports receives the long bottle aging needed for the Portuguese vintage or crusted port.

American white ports are made in essentially the same fashion, except that there is no problem with color extraction and even less attention paid to aging; they usually leave the winery the same year that they are made. Most are simply labeled *white port*, but a few wines with unique characteristics are sold under different names. These include *Muscatel*, usually made from the muscat of alexandria grape and Angelica, that is intensely sweet. Thompson Seedless grapes are among the principal varieties used to make white port.

Finally, there are a number of specialty wines that are classed with the more traditional ports because of their method of manufacture. California Tokay, for example, is a blend of red and white ports, mixed with sweet sherry, but it bears no relationship to the Tokay wines of Hungary.

Vermouth is not yet a popular drink in

A California state inspector takes a core sample of freshly picked grapes to gauge their sugar content and other key characteristics. These grapes will be used to make Tokay wine

the U.S. Although its use might be expected to increase along with that of the natural wines, vermouth sales have stayed at about one-eighth of the declining market for fortified wines. In Europe, the vermouths are a widely appreciated aperitif and are available in many styles. But U.S. vintners make vermouths almost exclusively for mixing with gin and whiskey, and this has limited the output and stifled their development as apéritifs.

The two basic kinds of vermouth made in this country are a pale dry white, sometimes labeled *French*, and a dark, sweet red, often called *Italian*; both are usually made from a neutral white port base. For

dry vermouth, the wine is reduced in color to look almost like gin and for sweet vermouth, color and caramel are added to make it attractive with whiskey. The herbs and spices infused in these wines are essentially the same as those used in making European vermouths, but as in France and Italy, each producer has his own combination of ingredients. The wines are normally fortified with grape brandy to an alcoholic strength of about 20 per cent.

Flavored Wines

This newest category of American wines first appeared in volume in the 1960s, and

produces only one wine from those grapes best suited to his individual soil, terrain and climate. For merchandising reasons U.S. vintners usually produce a much broader line of wines. Inevitably, American wineries must buy semi-finished wines from one another to add to those that they have made in insufficient quantity or to fill out their line with wines they cannot make themselves. Such wines are labelled *made and bottled* if at least 10 per cent of the grapes came from the producer's property. If the wine was simply bought from another producer for resale it must be labeled *cellared and bottled* or, simply, *bottled*.

Until recently, most U.S. vintners avoided the European practice of vintage labeling on the grounds that 'every year is a good year'. It is true that growing conditions are more stable, particularly in California, than in many of the world's major wine-growing areas. Nonetheless, American vineyards are no strangers to the droughts, downpours, frosts, hail, fire, insects and labor problems that account for poor grape crops elsewhere.

U.S. vintners have sought to moderate their inevitable variations in their production by blending the output of different years. Their goal, along with others in the American food and beverage industries, has been to market a product known for consistent quality. This policy has good and bad aspects. On the plus side, it puts the producer's business on a more stable basis and offers the customer an exceptionally dependable wine at a steady price; the debit side to this practice is that very little genuinely exciting wine has been reaching the its vocabulary has yet to be fully developed. Essentially, these wines are made from low quality, bulk production grapes, like the Thompson Seedless, that provide a base wine of neutral character. After fermentation, a number of non-grape additives are used to give flavor to the wine, and sometimes to provide effervescence or additional alcoholic strength. The most common flavorings are fruits such as apples, oranges, lemons, limes, grapefruit and various berries. Those wines that are carbonated or have an alcohol content of more than 14 per cent are sometimes referred to as 'flavored wines plus'.

So far there has been no attempt to develop standard terms for these wines similar to the generic/varietal system. Flavored wines are sold by proprietary names that are largely intended to appeal to the young adult population that constitutes the primary market. Examples include Thunderbird, Ripple, Boone's Apple Farm, Strawberry Hill, Annie Greensprings and I Luv You.

Frivolous as these names may sound, the sale of such 'pop' wines has become substantial, about 12 per cent of the total U.S. market. The implications for the future of American natural wine are not necessarily all bad. Until these fruit-flavored beverages came along, it was difficult for many Americans to develop a taste for wine. The most common introduction was through rosé wine, but even this least vinous of the traditional wines failed to attract some palates. Since the success of the revolution in American winemaking ultimately depends upon a significant number of Americans crossing over to the world of natural wine, the introduction of the pop varieties may prove to be one of the wine industry's most important assets.

The Vineyards of the West

California dominates the wine scene in both the western states and the whole U.S. Of the 400 million gallons of wine sold in this country in 1977, 286 million came from California, 46 million from all other states and 68 million from abroad. This means that three out of every four glasses of wine drunk here comes from California. California has more than 600,000 acres of wine grapes and about 350 commercial wine producers. In

Grape harvests in California are now insufficient to meet the increased public demand, but expanding the acreage may solve the problem in the next ten years

addition to a complete range of flavored, fortified, sparkling and generic wines, California vintners now offer more than 50 varietals.

The recent expansion of the California wine industry has no parallel in world vinicultural history. In the decade 1968–77 the state's wine grape bearing acreage increased by about 450,000 acres. Massive investment in new wineries and equipment has accompanied this huge vineyard growth. Much of the capital has come from the major corporations that have been taking over and expanding established vineyards. But a substantial number of new wineries have sprung up, some of which provide

good evidence that the growth in the California wine industry is one of quality as well as output. Their owners are emulating the methods of the top European vineyards and concentrating on only a few estate-bottled, vintage-dated varietal wines.

But the California wine scene is not entirely sunny. Chief among its problems is the cost of its products. Americans are largely unaware of the colossal investment undertaken by the California wine industry in response to their demand for more and better wines. Somehow they expect this demand to be met and at the same time believe that domestic wines should remain, as they

Early spring plowing in Sonoma Valley, California

were for so many years, a relatively inexpensive alternative to foreign vintages. The fact is that U.S. wines have lost their price advantage over imports of comparable quality and in some markets have become even more expensive than their foreign counterparts.

This development is attributable to several factors. The first is the enormous investment in expansion and improvement of the California wine industry already described; paying off the debts incurred in this effort demands a higher price on every bottle. The past decade has also seen a marked increase in operating costs; e.g., when wineries that paid $275 a ton for premium red wine grapes one year must pay $1,000 a ton

for the same grapes four years later, prices have to rise. Finally, inflation and as yet unabated customer demand for the improved wines coming from California have played their part in boosting retail prices.

Major Vineyards of the West
California wines are produced in three main regions: the northern coastal area around San Francisco Bay, the Great Central Valley, and in southern California near Los Angeles. Each of these regions is distinct in its climate, soil, viticulture and styles of wine.

The northern coastal region is the most prestigious in the nation. It is concentrated in the hills and valleys surrounding

San Francisco and consists of six districts, two north, two east and two south of the Bay. Grapes do not grow so abundantly in this region as they do in the Central Valley, but cool climate, hillside planting and natural irrigation make their quality comparable to those of the better European vineyards.

The Northern Coastal Region: Sonoma and Napa
It is appropriate to begin with the Sonoma Valley, the site of Haraszthy's pioneering work. Both natural and sparkling wines are made here and they vary significantly in style and quality because of surprising differences in climate within so small an area. The Sonoma district encompasses three of California's five climatic zones for wine-growing within its borders. The southern end of the valley has a cool climate (Zone II). There, the first major vineyard, driving from south to north, is Buena Vista, that remained in the Haraszthy family until 1906. In the 1940's the winery was restored and today it is best known for its Zinfandel, the popular and prolific red varietal that Haraszthy probably introduced to this country.

The Sebastiani winery is nearby; it makes a broad range of natural wines — the best of which are reds in the Italian style, particularly Barbera. Just to the north lies Hanzell vineyards, one of the relatively new firms that specializes in high-quality varietals. Modeled on Burgundy's renowned Clos de Vougeot, Hanzell concentrates on wines made from chardonnay and pinot noir grapes, the classical varieties used in France's Burgundy region.

Twenty miles further north, around the town of Santa Rosa, temperatures rise to moderate (Zone III); the principal vineyards here are Martini & Prati and Robert Lasdin. Towards the western edge of the valley, however, there is an abrupt shift back to very cool temperatures (Zone I). In this favored spot stands the Korbel winery, a firm that has specialized in sparkling wines since the 1860's. Its bottle-fermented champagne is among the finest made in the U.S.

Continuing north to Healdsburg, the climate reverts to moderate and here there are several small wineries including

High quality varietal wines being aged in small oak casks at the Simi Winery, Sonoma Valley

Foppiano, Cambiaso, Sonoma and Simi. The most interesting, Sonoma and Simi are the creations of relative newcomers to the wine industry. Sonoma, under the direction of former professional dancer Rod Strong, is a spectacularly modern winery producing good to high quality generic and varietal wines with an emphasis on finding the ideal micro-climate for each grape. Simi is an old but heretofore relatively unknown vineyard

that began to gain national recognition under the energetic leadership of a former oil industry leader, Russ Green. Simi's investments in new production equipment and attention to quality have made it a frontrunner.

North of Healdsburg, the climate gets progressively warmer. The principal wineries are Pedrocelli, Rege, Parducci and Italian Swiss Colony. The latter is the largest firm in this district and one of

the largest in California. Its Sonoma Valley vineyards at Asti are only a small part of the firm's state-wide production that covers almost the whole range of wines. Their natural generic wines are good value for the money.

The Napa district lies parallel and to the east of the Sonoma Valley and its climate is marginally cooler than Sonoma. From north to south, the parade of famous vineyards begins with

The Christian Brothers winery at St. Helena in the Napa Valley

two celebrated champagne producers, Kornell and Schramsberg. Hans Kornell's fine wines are often confused with those of Korbel in the Sonoma Valley and, in fact, the two firms' sparkling wines are similar.

Schramsberg enjoyed considerable renown in the 19th century, but was abandoned after the founder's death in 1905. It has recently been revived by Jack Davies who already appears to have out-classed all other U.S. champagne makers. Moreover, he believes it is only a beginning and that, in the future, American sparkling wines could rival the world's finest.

Just south of Schramsberg are two small wineries specializing in natural varietals. On the east side of the valley, Souverain produces some distinguished whites (such as Johannisberg Riesling), and the Stony Hill winery makes a Chardonnay that is among the finest whites in America.

The next cluster of wineries includes Freemark, Abbey, Christian Brothers, Berringer and Charles Krug. Krug, operated since 1943 by the Mondavi family, has been remarkably successful in combining quality and quantity to produce a broad range of generic and varietal wines. Christian Brothers is a Catholic monastery that makes wines to support its schools and colleges throughout the U.S. Its large winery at St. Helena specializes in bulk process sparkl-

ing wines and there are several Christian Brothers vineyards in Napa and other wine districts that produce natural and fortified wines as well as brandy.

South of St. Helena come the Sutter Home Winery, the Sunny St. Helena Winery, and of special interest, Heitz Wine Cellars and the Louis M. Martini winery. Joe Heitz has been producing wines under his own name only since the early 1960's, but he served a long apprenticeship in the profession and is regarded as one of the best vintners of the Napa Valley. He makes both generic and varietal wines; the best include his Cabernet Sauvignon, Pinot Noir and Chardonnay.

A high-quality producer for decades,

Mid-summer vine-tending in the Inglenook vineyards in the Napa Valley

Louis M. Martini is sometimes called the dean of California vintners. His generics have long been excellent and his varietals, seldom equalled in quality until recently, include a fine Zinfandel and Cabernet Sauvignon.

At Rutherford, the climate becomes very cool (Zone I) and the Napa Valley ends with some particularly distinguished names: Beaulieu Vineyards, Inglenook, Chappellet and Robert Mondavi. Beaulieu and Inglenook are Napa Valley landmarks with a long established reputation. In the 1960's, they were bought by the Heublein Corporation as the showpieces of its new wine empire and Heublein has been careful to maintain their individuality.

Chappellet is a striking new winery in the hills on the eastern side of the Napa Valley. It makes a few top-quality wines, notably Chardonnay and Cabernet Sauvignon.

At Robert Mondavi's winery, the focus is on varietal wines and advanced vinicultural techniques. Mondavi has been among the most perceptive and audacious of California vintners in employing new methods and equipment and his winery is a showplace for the industry. His Cabernet Sauvignon is among the state's finest and his transformation of California's formerly lackluster Sauvignon Blanc into the new Fumé Blanc varietal is a great achievement.

The Northern Coastal Region: East Bay and Livermore

East of San Francisco Bay lie the less well-known wine districts of Alameda and Contra Costa counties and the Livermore Valley. The climate of the East Bay counties is cool; wineries here include Weibel, Lords & Elwood, Davis Bynum, Conrad Viano and Digardi. With the exception of the Weibel winery, started by Governor Leland Stanford in 1869, these wineries produce largely for the local market. Urbanization and land scarcity has forced most of them to buy their grapes from other growers and some have moved their wineries to more rural areas, leaving only sales outlets in the East Bay.

The gravelly soil in the Livermore Valley vineyards is well-suited to producing white wines

Just over the coastal range from the East Bay district lies the Livermore Valley. Again, the number of vineyards is not large and the vintners must contend not only with urbanization, but also with a warm Zone III climate. However, the valley floor is composed of a rough, quick-draining gravel very similar to that found in Bordeaux. This allows Livermore vintners to make the finest American wines in the Graves and Sauternes styles.

The top vineyard of the Livermore Valley is Wente Brothers, now run by the family's fourth generation in California. This vineyard produces a broad range of wines, but is best known for its white varietals. Wente's Dry Sémillon is the best Californian white Graves and they also produce a remarkable Sauternes type wine, made partly from vines from

France's famous Château d'Yquem. Wente also makes a commendable, reasonably priced Chardonnay.

The Concannon Vineyard next door is smaller but equally impressive. Founded in 1884, only a year after Wente Brothers, it also specializes in high-quality, white varietals. Other Livermore Valley producers include Villa Armando and Ruby Hill.

The Northern Coastal Region: Santa Clara and Monterey

The last two districts of the Northern Coastal region are Santa Clara/Santa Cruz and Monterey/San Benito. Santa Clara is just south of San Francisco Bay and includes some of the oldest vineyards in the state, while Monterey, 60 miles further south, is California's newest

winemaking area. Both districts offer vintners good growing conditions, classified as Zones I and II.

The urban sprawl of San José is encroaching on the Santa Clara Valley, so its vineyards tend to be crowded against the Santa Cruz mountains to the west and the Diabolo range to the east. Those along the western edge of the valley include such well-known firms as Almaden, Paul Masson and the Jesuit seminary and vineyard, Novitiate of Los Gatos, that makes sacramental and other wines to support its teaching activities.

Almaden was founded at Los Gatos in 1852 and today is one of the largest makers of good quality generics and varietals, as well as naturally fermented sparkling wines, solera-process fortified wines and brandy. It was bought by the

National Distillers Corporation in 1967. Paul Masson is similar to Almaden in many respects. Founded in the 1880s, the winery is known for an enormous inventory of all types of wines. It was sold to the Seagram's Company in 1943 and still continues to grow.

High in the hills above the Santa Clara Valley are three small producers specializing in a few classic varietals. Martin Ray began making quality wines in the 1940's, Ridge Vineyard in 1962 and David Bruce in 1964. Each are different in their interests and techniques, but all may be described as perfectionists and dedicated to making California wines at a new level of excellence.

On the east side of the Santa Clara Valley are the vineyards of Mirassou, Richert, San Martin, Live Oaks, Bonesio and Bertero. Mirassou is by far the most important, with national distribution of its generic and varietal wines and a reputation as a pioneer in vinicultural technology. It has had particular success with less well-established varietals, including the Pinot Blanc, Chenin Blanc and Petit Sirah.

The Monterey district offers an exciting new opportunity for California winemakers. Its potential as a vineyard area was not perceived until the University of California survey of grape-growing conditions indicated that Monterey was in climatic Zones I and II. Initial experience suggests that this district may be even better for wine than the Napa Valley. Only time will show, but new vineyards have been laid out in this district at a record rate during the past 10 years and the new acreage is already more than half that of the Napa Valley. Most important, these vineyards are being planted almost exclusively with the highest quality grape varieties.

Nearly all the Monterey vintners are long-established firms which have expanded beyond their original districts. They include Almaden, Paul Masson, Mirassou and Wente Brothers. Their new vineyards are concentrated in the Salinas Valley between Soledad and King City, and along the San Andreas Rift between Hollister and Paicines. The sole original Monterey vineyard is Chalone; this tiny property in the Gabilan Range above Soledad specializes in Chardonnay and Pinot Noir varietals.

Vineyard workers gather the harvest from the Santa Clara Valley, California

High quality vineyards are clustered in the western hills overlooking the Santa Clara Valley

The Great Central Valley

The Central Valley's three districts of Lodi/Sacramento, Escalon/Modesto and Fresno/San Joaquin produce 75 per cent of the state's wine. This enormous production is made possible by steady sunshine, miles of flat, fertile terrain and extensive irrigation; the climate ranges from warm to hot (Zones IV and V).

For many years, the wineries of this region concentrated on bulk production of cheap, fortified wines. These products still constitute a significant proportion of their total output. But in recent years, the winemakers of the Central Valley have accomplished a remarkable alteration of their industry in response to the public's demand for more and better natural wines. These innovative vintners turned to new, heat-resistant strains of natural wine grapes developed by the University of California. They made massive use of refrigeration equipment and stainless steel and developed new techniques for making better quality generic wines in larger quantities and in a shorter time than had been thought possible at home or abroad.

The result of this monumental effort is that the U.S. already enjoys what is probably the best and most consistently made 'vin ordinaire' in the world. In a sense, this is the first great achievement of the American wine revolution, since it involves the wine that most people drink most of the time: the generics. For the foreseeable future, Central Valley natural wine production will be mainly generic, unless some startling advance improves the heat resistance of the thoroughbred grapes required to make varietal wines. The Central Valley's success with generic wines may have the added benefit of pushing the Northern Coastal region more and more into varietal production.

The northernmost of the Great Central Valley's three districts is Lodi/Sacramento. Here a combination of large and small producers, including Barengo, East Side, Alexander, Lockeford, Gibson and Guild, make both natural and fortified wines. Barengo is noted for its Ruby Cabernet, a new varietal which is the result of cross-breeding the Cabernet Sauvignon with the carignan grape for better yield and heat resistance. Guild is one of the larger producers in the Central Valley and makes an enormous range of natural, sparkling and fortified wines; its

Italian-style, generic red is popular.

The next district, Escalon/Modesto, is the home of the three giants of California winemaking: Gallo, Franzia and Petri. Gallo is by far the largest producer in the state and makes more than one out of every three glasses of wine drunk in the U.S. Its plant is a technological wonder, looking more like an oil refinery than a winery, and is renowned throughout the trade; no single firm has done more to upgrade the quality of Central Valley production than Gallo. Franzia makes a full line of natural and fortified wines and it is also establishing a reputation for bulk-process sparkling wines.

The third district of Fresno/San Joaquin is the home of more large-volume producers like Roma and Cribari. The most distinguished firm, in terms of quality, is Ficklin, concentrating on high-quality ports. Unique among California's fortified wine producers, Ficklin employs the classic grape varieties and winemaking methods of Portugal. Unfortunately, its wines are not regularly distributed outside of California.

These vineyards typify the flat land and the hot weather growing conditions prevailing in the Great Central Valley, California

Southern California

Winemaking in the southern region has not progressed with the rest of the American winemaking industry. A revival may still be possible, but the area's vineyards are threatened by urban development and air pollution. Moreover, its principal product is the sweet, fortified wines that are losing popularity.

Nevertheless, a number of wineries continue to operate in this region, most of them grouped around the town of Cucamonga. Gallo and Guild maintain production and distribution centers in this area. The local firms include Abbona, Brookside, Cherpin, Cucamonga, Filippi, Regina and Thomas. Most of the natural wines these firms produce are generics, but there are a few varietals, the best of which reflect the Italian heritage of many of the area's vintners.

Other Western Vineyards

The wine output of the other western states is tiny, but may increase substantially in the future. In the southwest, small plantings of good quality grapes have been made in Arizona and New Mexico, but the real center of growth is in the Pacific Northwest states of Washington and Oregon.

Washington State's potential as a wine-growing area has long been known, but serious development only began in the mid-1960s when the demand for wine increased. East of the Cascade Range, the climate is similar to New York State and there is ample suitable land. So far the soil is free of phylloxera and other root diseases, making Washington one of the few areas of the world where *vitis vinifera* grapes can be grown directly on their own roots. Like New York, however, Washington's severe winters can adversely affect the delicate *vinifera* wine and the French-American grape varieties may have more lasting promise.

The new vineyards are centered around the town of Grandview in the Yakima Valley and the major producers are Boordy Vineyards, the Seneca Foods Corporation and American Wine Growers (labeled Ste. Michele). Boordy and Ste. Michele have limited national distribution; varietals include Cabernet Sauvignon, Chardonnay, Gamay, Gewürztraminer, Pinot Blanc and Pinot Noir.

In Oregon, growing conditions are less conducive to large-scale production. Its vintners believe however that they will be able to produce better wines than Washington since climate studies show that the weather is comparable to some of the best districts of northern Europe. The best wines are likely to be the classic white varietals made from *vinifera* grapes.

Oregon's vineyards are concentrated in the Willamette Valley around Roseburg. The most highly developed vineyard is the Hillcrest Winery, owned by Richard Sommers. His most successful wine is the Johannisburg Riesling, but he is also working with chardonnay, gewürztraminer, sémillon and sauvignon blanc grapes. Other wineries growing *vinifera* grapes include the Paul Bjelland vineyard near Rosebury, Eyrie Vineyards at Dundee and the Charles Coury Vineyards in Forest Grove.

The Vineyards of the East

Nowhere is the necessity — and the opportunity — for change in American winemaking so compelling as in the eastern states. For more than a century, the wine industry of this part of the country has been considered the also-ran of U.S. viniculture. Hobbled by an inhospitable environment, it has had to run the race on hardy, native stock — grapes that many people feel should not be used for making wine.

Despite this fundamental handicap, it has limped along. It has done so by concentrating on sparkling and fortified wines in which the peculiar bouquet and

U.S. Bonded Winery No. 1 — The Great Western Wine Company of Hammondsport, New York

The laborious process of grafting European grapestock to American roots is necessary because of phylloxera and other soil diseases

Eastern winemakers may also be able to grow variants of the classic European wine vines. Grafting to American root stock can protect them from soil diseases; new sprays and vine-tending techniques offer ways of protecting the stalks, leaves and fruit; most important, hardier strains of vines have been developed by progressive propagation from *vinifera* vines that have shown a capacity to withstand the rigors of the eastern climate.

These promising developments with *vinifera* and French-American grapes do not mean that every native vine should be thrown out of native vineyards. Some of the original American wines have genuine merit as well as historical interest and it would be a pity if they were to disappear. Their sweet, grapey characteristics are still appreciated and, like California's pop wines, may help to introduce more people to wine. Moreover, new methods of vinification suggest that the aroma and unsophisticated flavor of the native wines can be moderated.

In the long run, however, the future for eastern winemaking must be chiefly based on European-type grapes. Most vintners accept this premise and many are replanting or setting out new vineyards, largely in the French-American vines. Some of the varieties now being planted can still be improved to produce grapes of greater hardiness and European character. A beginning has been made and it seems likely that the revolution in eastern wines will be at least as dramatic as that already under way in the West.

Major Vineyards of the East

Most eastern vineyards are planted near lakes because of their moderating effect of a surrounding air temperature. The greatest concentration of eastern vineyards is around the Finger Lakes of central New York State. The four largest of these lakes are long, narrow and deep, running 30 miles or more from north to south. Their steep, quick-draining western hillsides offer rocky, mineral-rich soil, good exposure to the morning sun and protection from cruel western winds. The setting is extraordinarily handsome, not unlike that of the Rhine.

The first known winemaker of this region was the Reverend William Bostwick, who set out vines in his parish garden at Hammondsport, on Lake

usually sweet taste of native grapes is not so evident. Its location has given it a competitive advantage over California and Europe in selling to this country's largest population centers. Until recently, it has been selling to a public of which not one in a hundred thousand recognized that eastern wines were made from basically different grapes than those used in making most other wines.

But now the public has become interested chiefly in natural wines; it has a wide range of Californian and European wines from which to choose and, increasingly, it can discern these wines from those made with native grape varieties.

It is a new ball game and the eastern vintners must change the way they play or, sooner or later, surrender the field.

Fortunately, this need not — and probably will not — happen. After more than three centuries of frustration with American vines, the winemakers of the East have been offered a solution full of practicality and promise: a wide range of new grapes with which to make wines that can compete with those from California and abroad.

Most of these new grapes are the previously described French-American varieties. But recent experimentation with *vitis vinifera* grape varieties suggests that

The original Taylor vineyards on the western slopes above Lake Keuka have an ideal location

region was the Reverend William Bostwick, who set out vines in his parish garden at Hammondsport, on Lake Keuka, in 1828. By mid-century, several small commercial vineyards, that were to form the nucleus of today's New York wine industry, had been established around this lake. Among the early companies that have survived are Great Western (1860), Gold Seal (1865) and Taylor (1880). Twenty miles to the west, on the shores of Lake Canandaigua, the Widmer Wine Company was established at Naples in 1882.

Taylor took over the Great Western winery in 1961 and is now the giant among eastern vintners. The separate identity of both organizations has been maintained, however. Taylor concentrates on generic wines and mass-produced sherries and ports, while Great Western mainly produces varietals and fortified solera wines. Both companies make the sparkling wines that have long been their best sellers. The purchase of Taylor in 1977 by the Coca-Cola Company seems to have set this old firm on a new course, one which reduces its exclusively eastern character. Increased use of hybrid grapes, blending of New York with California wines, and a new line of 'Taylor California' wines reportedly are involved.

Gold Seal still makes many of its wines from native grapes and concentrates on the sparkling and fortified types in which traditional eastern grape flavors are least apparent. But this company deserves credit for being the first to experiment with both French-American and *vinifera* vines in the 1940's and continues to make a few top quality wines from these varieties. Gold Seal does not yet appear to have committed itself to wines based on European grapes, but its long experience in this field should prove invaluable.

Widmer is another eastern wine company whose public image is of the old school. Its wines are among the most unabashedly eastern on the market today and it produces certain varietals that are

Johannisberg Riesling vines flourish in Dr. Konstantin Frank's Vinifera Vineyards in New York State

available from no other major winery. But public images can be deceptive. In the late 1960s Widmer became part of a major food products company and has gained the capital to expand in new directions. It made large plantings of French-American hybrid stock, but more important, it broke ground for a new 500-acre vineyard in California in 1960. This move has made Widmer what might be called the first 'national' wine company and should provide it with the red wines that eastern vintners have found so difficult to produce from native stock.

In the 1960s two Finger Lakes vineyards were established with differing goals that are of major importance for the future of eastern winemaking. Both are small properties located high on the western shore of Lake Keuka. They are devoted entirely to the cultivation of high-quality grape stock with which to make estate bottled, vintage-dated wines that can demonstrate the ultimate potential of viniculture in the East. Their owners are considered unorthodox, even radical, by other eastern vintners. But their zeal and accomplishments are widely respected and the significantly higher standards they have set for themselves seem certain to benefit the whole eastern wine industry.

The first of these new vineyards is the creation of Dr. Konstantin Frank, a dedicated viticulturalist who believes that with proper techniques *vinifera* grapes can be made to grow widely in the East. Moreover, he holds that the Finger Lakes are inherently better for growing these classic varieties than California. The white wines from his appropriately named Vinifera Vineyards are certainly among the finest yet produced in the U.S., but so far most eastern growers ascribe their success to Frank's personal skills and dedication and are unwilling to gamble extensively on *vinifera* grapes. Nevertheless, this extraordinary man has blazed a new trail which suggests that even hardier strains of *vinifera* can be developed that will make it more attractive for the big producers to follow in his footsteps.

The other new vineyard of key importance is Bully Hill. The site is that of the original Taylor Wine Company and the owner is Walter Taylor, grandson of its founder but no longer connected with

Taylor-Great Western. At Bully Hill, wines are made from native, French-American and *vinifera* grapes and the guiding principle is that the less that is done to a wine while it is being made, the better. This return to naturalism in eastern winemaking is Walter Taylor's reaction to years of first-hand experience with the techniques generally used to compensate for the deficiencies of native grapes and a harsh climate. Bully Hill has become something of a gadfly to the eastern industry by exposing the way that traditional wines are doctored with heat, chemicals, water, sugar, salt and up to 25 per cent California wine without declaration on the label. Its owner argues that the future for New York wine lies in throwing away such crutches and turning to better grapes and winery procedures.

Other Eastern Vineyards
Eastern winemaking is by no means confined to the Finger Lakes. Vineyards exist elsewhere in New York as well as in Illinois, Georgia, Virginia, South Carolina, Ohio, Michigan and Arkansas (to name the top producers in order) plus 28 other states. Of all these sources of eastern wine, however, perhaps the most important are New York, Ohio and Maryland.

In New York there are three other producers of note in the Finger Lakes region: Canandaigua Industries, Boordy Vineyard and the Hammondsport Winery. In the Hudson River Valley, the Brotherhood Winery, High Tor Vineyard and the Hudson Valley Wine Company make a wide range of wines, chiefly from native grapes. In western New York, near Lake Erie, Boordy Vineyard, Niagara Falls Wine Company and the Monarch Wine Company (Manischewitz) work with native and French-American varieties.

Ohio's most successful vineyards are on small islands, offshore from Sandusky, in Lake Erie.

Maryland holds a special place in the eastern wine picture because it is the home of Philip Wagner's original Boordy Vineyard near Baltimore. Wagner was the first to realize the potential of French-American grapes and he began experimenting with them in the 1930s. Objectively tasted, his wines are no better than any good 'vin ordinaire' from Europe or California, but this represents a striking accomplishment compared to most eastern wines. But Wagner's greatest achievement lies in the development of French-American grape stock for other vintners. Boordy vines are now planted throughout the East and as far away as the Pacific Northwest. If it turns out that these grapes give the wine industry of this part of the country the new lease on life that many now foresee, Wagner, like Haraszthy in California, may find himself being referred to as the 'Father of Modern Eastern Viniculture'.

The Greyton H. Taylor Wine Museum in Hammondsport, N. Y. The buildings housed the original Taylor Wine Company from 1883 to 1920.

Glasses for Wine

Serving wine successfully begins with good glassware. Over the years, the most important wine regions have developed distinctive glasses as well as characteristic bottles intended to accentuate the virtues of their wines. A selection of such specialized glasses is illustrated here. They can be a pleasure to collect and use, but they are a luxury rather than a necessity. One set of glassware will do for all wines, if its design assists the eye and the nose as well as the palate to appreciate all that any wine has to offer. What is needed are a few, clear, amply-proportioned, stemmed glasses that are narrow at the top.

Wine must be seen, as well as sniffed and savored. A wine's color, clarity and density provide important clues to its origin, age and condition. More important, the play of light on this many-hued beverage is a pleasure in itself. For all these reasons, wine should be served in clear, simply designed glasses. Tinted, convoluted or elaborately engraved vessels only take away from one of the basic satisfactions wine affords — its appearance.

A wine glass should also make it easy to enjoy the scent of a wine — connoisseurs consider it almost as important as taste itself. The way to make the most of a wine's scent is to use a glass large enough so that when a generous portion is poured the glass will still be only half full. This permits the wine's aroma to concentrate in the upper half of the glass, where it can be fully appreciated. The effect is intensified if the glass is slightly narrow at the top, slowing the dissipation of the wine's bouquet into the air. Ideally, glasses should have a minimum capacity of six ounces so that a normal three-ounce serving will still leave room for the scent to gather and be enjoyed to the full.

Finally, a good wine glass should have a stem. Stemmed glassware is more attractive than a tumbler, but the real reason for the stem is to keep the warmth of the hand from touching the body of the glass.

Plain, simple wine glasses (top). Rare 18th-century twisted stem wine glasses centre and below a selection of rare wine glasses

Preparing the Bottle

There is no great trick to preparing a bottle of wine for serving. If at all possible, it should come to the table after a prolonged rest in the cellar, so the wine has had time to shake off any ill effects of its travels. If the wine is red, it is wise to bring it from the cellar a day or so in advance and stand it upright. This permits it to assume the 'room temperature' at which reds are usually served and allows any sediment to settle.

A few red wines — notably old Burgundies and vintage ports — have considerable sediment. After this harmless material collects at the bottom of a bottle, it can be easily separated by pouring the wine into another clean, glass container, leaving the dregs in the original bottle. This process, called 'decanting', demands only a steady hand, a sharp eye and the courage to sacrifice the last inch or so of wine. A good source of light near the neck of the bottle will help spot the sediment before it flows into the new container.

Most reds do not require decanting, but some people do it regularly to aerate the wine and let it toss off any mustiness it may have developed in the bottle. Much the same effect can be gained more simply by drawing the cork an hour or two before the wine is to be used. This is called 'letting the wine breathe'.

White wines require no decanting or breathing. Made without skins and other grape solids, they throw no sediment and do not seem to benefit from aeration. They are improved by cooling, however. An ice bucket can be used, but sudden chilling tends to numb the wine and makes it less attractive. How cold to serve a white wine is a matter of personal preference, but most people serve them too chilled, which diminishes the wine's bouquet and flavor. Dry white wines seem best between 50° and 55° and the sweeter types between 45° and 50°. For cooling, treat rosé wines as whites.

Silver mounted glass bottle, decanter, in the Victoria and Albert Museum, London (top). Wine glass beautifully engraved with a bird cage (left), and the single bottle of wine and plain glasses in which the wine can be enjoyed to the full

139

Opening and Pouring

With proper glasses on hand and the bottle prepared, all that remains is to open and pour. There are a wide variety of openers on the market today and each has its partisans. If you use the traditional corkscrew, the screw should be broad enough to take a firm hold on the cork and there should be some sort of leverage device to make the pulling easier. It is also helpful to have a small knife attachment with which to peel away the lead foil and any deposits covering the bottle opening. After the cork is drawn, the lip should be wiped clean.

By tradition the host pours the first portion in his glass so that any remaining residue or bits of cork will not be served to his guests; it also gives him a chance to check that the wine is up to standard. A twist of the bottle after each pouring will prevent dripping and a napkin is often used to assure a better grip on a chilled bottle. However, the label should not be permanently obscured; when everyone is served the bottle should be left in view — a custom that applies even when the wine has been decanted. If more than one kind of wine is served, it is usual to serve white before red, dry before sweet, young before old, light before full-bodied and an average wine before one of exalted reputation.

A selection of openers, the 'traditional' type (dated 1917) with a broad screw to hold the cork firmly, and above it a corkscrew with lever and blade attachments. Below, a candle below the neck of the bottle makes it easier to see when the sediment in the wine reaches the neck. Right, the best known traditional shapes and sizes of bottles

Sparkling Wines

The service of sparkling wines is a subject to itself. Champagne and its lesser cousins differ from other wines in their effervescence — bubbles of carbon-dioxide gas that give a sensation of liveliness on the palate when the wine is drunk. Until that moment, the host should take every precaution to see that these valuable bubbles are preserved.

'Traditional' Champagne glasses seem diabolically designed to spoil sparkling wines. Their wide mouths permit the rapid escape of effervescence, leaving the wine flat and insipid. A standard wine glass is far better and the best choice is the tall, slim 'flute' or 'tulip' glass used in Champagne.

Sparkling wines should be chilled to between 40° and 45° to slow the action of the bubbles. To avoid agitating the gas, the bottle should be handled gently. After removing the wire pressure guard and foil from the neck of the bottle, the cork should be eased — not blasted — out. To do this, wrap one hand in a napkin, then grip and slowly twist the cork; with the other hand, turn the bottle in the opposite direction, and draw it away from the cork. A discreet 'pop' is enough; flying corks may provide some amusement, but they dissipate the bubbles that are the heart of Champagne.

Bottle Shapes and Sizes

For many years, the principal vinicultural regions of Europe have used specially-shaped bottles that have come to be associated with their wines. Increasingly, the newer vinicultural nations are adopting the same bottle shapes for similar wines. Thus, even when labels are obscure, a knowledge of bottle shapes can give a rough guide to the wines they contain. Here are some of the best-known traditional shapes and sizes:

CHAMPAGNE

Champagne is normally bottled in a very stout glass bottle holding 1 pint 11 fluid ounces. There is a series of special bottles including:

Magnum – equal to 2 bottles or 3 pints and 6 fl. oz.

Jeroboam – equal to 4 bottles or 3 quarts and 12 fl. oz.

Rehoboam – equal to 6 bottles or 1 gallon, 1 quart and 2 fl. oz.

Methusalah – equal to 8 bottles or 1 gallon, 2 quarts, 1 pint and 4 fl. oz.

Salamanazar – equal to 12 bottles or 2 gallons, 2 quarts and 4 fl. oz.

Balthazar – equal to 16 bottles or 3 gallons, 1 quart, 1 pint and 1 fl. oz.

Nebuchadnezzar – equal to 20 bottles or 4 gallons, 1 pint and 13 fl. oz.

Champagne must have been one of the first liquids ever to be sold in non-returnable bottles. The high internal pressure maintained inside the bottle is too much of a strain on the glass for it to be used a second time.

BORDEAUX

Bordeaux wines, both red and white, are bottled in narrow, 'square-shouldered' bottles. They have the advantage of stacking easily and the wine can be poured almost to the last without any sediment passing beyond the shoulder. Dark green glass is used for red wines and clear for white. In addition to standard 24 ounce bottles, Bordeaux wines come in 'Fillettes' (half bottles). Magnums (2 bottles), Marie-Jeannes (3 bottles), Double Magnums (4 bottles), Jeroboams (6 bottles) and Imperials (8 bottles).

BURGUNDY

The traditional bottle is 'soft-shouldered', sloping gracefully from the neck to a fairly full body. Red wines are usually bottled in dark green glass and the glass for whites is of a lighter shade. In addition to standard bottles holding 24 ounces, Burgundy wines are sometimes sold in 12 ounce half-bottles and Magnums containing 48 ounces.

BEAUJOLAIS

Most Beaujolais is shipped in traditional Burgundy bottles. Some producers, however, also offer a 'pot' bottle in either full size (24 ounces) or ¾ size (16 ounces).

LOIRE

The bottles are very similar to those of Burgundy but the taper from neck to body is more gradual and the glass is usually a paler shade of green. Rosé wines are often sold in clear glass bottles with somewhat longer necks.

RHONE

Most are shipped in Burgundy-type bottles. Those from Châteauneuf-du-Pape are often embossed with the papal seal. However, in an effort to distinguish their wines from those of Burgundy, some producers of Rhône wines have recently begun using a squat, square-shouldered bottle.

ALSACE

These wines are usually sold in bottles called 'flutes' that have a long, tapering neck and are made of light green glass.

GERMAN

The bottles are similar to those of Alsace, but the necks are not quite so long. The Rheingau district usually favors brown glass bottles, while those from the Mosel use green glass. One exception to the standard German bottles is the 'bocksbeutal' of the Franconia district that resembles a small flask.

ITALIAN

These come in a wide variety of shapes and sizes, the most familiar being the raffia-covered Chianti bottle.

AMERICAN

U.S. bottle shapes tend to conform to those of the famous wine regions of France and Germany, e.g., Cabernet Sauvignon comes in Bordeaux-style bottles and Johannisberg Riesling comes in a Rhine-style bottle. The main difference is that standard American bottles are slightly larger (25.6 ounces) than the average European bottle (24 ounces).

The Home Wine Cellar

There are many good reasons for keeping at least a modest supply of wine at home. Three are compelling: convenience, economy and improved quality in the wines you serve. Happily, this is one home project which can be carried out without any outside help.

Too many people buy their wines at the last moment before a dinner party, hastily selecting only those bottles they estimate are needed for that particular meal. With an adequate cache of wines at home, such irksome last-minute trips can be avoided; moreover, if a bad wine or unexpected guests turn up, there is a ready reserve to turn to for an extra bottle. Finally, for it is a pleasure as well as a convenience (not only when there is company) to be able to reach for that special bottle with which to celebrate good news or to indulge that sudden wish for a taste of fine wine.

With a place to store bottles at home, you can take the following steps significantly to reduce the cost of buying wine. First, buy in quantity. Nearly all stores offer some discount on case lots (12 bottles), usually taking about 10 per cent off the individual bottle price. Some merchants also give savings on smaller lots, such as half cases or even three bottles of the same wine.

Second, watch for sales. The vagaries of wholesale distribution are such that wine retailers are often overstocked with certain vintages and will offer them at bargain prices to gain shelf space. Sometimes the retailer is in need of ready cash to finance a new shipment. Whatever the reason, sales are not uncommon in the wine trade and, with a place to put away your purchases, you are ready to capitalize on discounts.

Third, buy wines when they are young. Any wine goes up in price as it grows older — even if its quality is not improving. Inflation is partly responsible, but market forces are also involved. As the trade supply of a well regarded wine diminishes, merchants who have a few remaining bottles can demand a higher price. For those wines that improve with age, prices increase as the bottle continues to occupy valuable storage space and improve in quality. By buying wines when they first arrive at the retail outlet and storing them at home you avoid this price escalation.

The owner of a cellar can also expect more satisfaction from his own wines than from those just brought from a shop. Wines are like people in many respects. Generally hardy, they can take a lot of knocks when young and still not suffer in their maturity. However, like people disorientated by sudden time changes of the jet age, wines are not well adapted to travel. Like humans, they usually recover in short order, but when drunk too soon after a trip they are not at their best.

This temporary diminution of a wine's quality varies with the length of the trip, the care it receives, and with the basic quality and age of the wine. A short drive home from the liquor store is unlikely to do much damage to a modest bottle of wine. But how is one to know that the same bottle didn't just arrive at the store after a 3,000 mile ocean voyage? How much better it is to serve wines that have had time to collect themselves in the cellar at home.

For all these reasons, it is a matter of prudence, not extravagance, to make room for wines at home. How much space is alotted will obviously depend upon the rate at which wine is consumed, financial constraints and the amount of space available. A cellar can be anything from a cardboard box to a panelled chamber. Its usefulness depends less upon its size than upon its success in providing the environment for maintaining wines in good condition.

Wine is a living thing, responsive to its surroundings, and one can go to great lengths to insure an ideal environment. Some people even install an air conditioner to keep their cellar at 55°F. — the temperature that permits white wines to live longer and reds to make that leisurely advance toward maturity that develops their finest qualities.

But such elaborate and expensive measures are not necessary. Most wines will survive and even improve anywhere that human beings are comfortable. The higher the temperature, the more quickly the wine will mature. But unless the bottles are exposed to near-freezing conditions or to one of those super-heated homes kept at above 75°F., there is little chance of spoilage. What wines really need is not so much one particular temperature, as a constant temperature.

The great enemy of wine is change, and this applies not only to temperature but also to humidity, light and position. This means that wines must not be subjected to blasts of hot and cold air, alternating sunlight and darkness, the slamming of doors and the vibration of home appliances. The kitchen, for example, is a popular place to keep wine, but with its periodic temperature changes and frenetic activity it is in fact one of the worst choices.

But there are any number of good places — even in the most active, modest household. All that is required is some secluded corner where conditions are reasonably stable. A space under the stairway will do; so will a bookcase in the study or a closet in the bedroom. The success of your cellar will depend less on its location than on the chance it affords your wines to rest in peace.

Once the site is chosen, all that remains is to provide some sort of space-saving arrangement for stacking the bottles so that they can lie on their sides. In a horizontal position the wine stays in contact with the cork and keeps it moist; a dry cork will shrink and permit vinegar-producing, airborne bacteria to reach the wine.

Wine shops and department stores offer a good selection of ready-made racks for home cellars, but they can be expensive. The wooden cases in which Bordeaux wines are still shipped are a good, no-cost alternative. You can also build a 'bookcase for wine' or install shelves in a closet, remembering to make some provision to keep the bottles from rolling about. Inexpensive and attractive storage bins have been made by stacking sections of ceramic drain pipe.

Obviously, nothing very complicated need be involved in developing a serviceable place to store wine at home. Once it is established, your only task — an agreeable one — is to keep it filled.

Wines stored in a simple rack in the 'European Wine Warehouse' in Holborn, London. There are many ready-made racks for home cellars on sale, although they tend to be expensive. The basic requirements are stable temperatures, humidity, light and position. A cupboard under the stairs, a bedroom closet, or a bookcase provide better conditions than anywhere in the kitchen